The Mailbox® Monthly Idea Books—Your Ultimate Monthly Resource!

Your friends at *The Mailbox®* have taken monthly books to a whole new level! We've created a Web site that contains even more classroom resources to complement the hundreds of curriculum-based activities in each book. We've also added skill lines to each idea for a quick curriculum reference at a glance. Plus, every book has a comprehensive index to make planning and selecting activities even easier! All of these terrific features make this series of monthly books one that you can't be without!

Now Internet Interactive!

- For each book, you'll enjoy over **50 pages** of online resources, such as patterns, reproducibles, transparency masters, and classroom forms!
- You'll find **new** resources for **every** thematic unit in each book!
- Many classroom forms can be **filled out online** and printed. No more handwritten versions!
- Web site content is tailored to you and your **grade level**.
- **All** reproducibles and pattern pages from each monthly book are available online for **easy printing.**
- Access is absolutely **FREE!**

Getting your online extras is as easy as 1, 2, 3!

1. Go to **www.themailboxbooks.com** and click on "Add a book."
2. Complete the simple registration form.
3. Follow the on-screen instructions to add your book.

Look for the computer icon 🖥 throughout each book to guide you to your FREE online extras.

From Your Friends at The MAILBOX®

About This Book

It's hard to believe we could improve on our best-selling series of monthly idea books—but we have! In this edition, you'll find the following exciting new features added to our irreplaceable collection of curriculum-based ideas!

- A Web site containing *even more* classroom resources complements the hundreds of activities provided in each book. (To access this incredible site for free, follow the simple instructions found on page 1.)
- A skill line for each idea provides a curriculum reference at a glance.
- A comprehensive index makes selecting and planning activities a breeze!

We think you'll agree that these new features make this series of monthly books the best ever!

Managing Editors: Cayce Guiliano, Scott Lyons
Editor at Large: Diane Badden
Contributing Writers: Becky Andrews, Lorraine Brandt, Caroline Chapman, Irving P. Crump, Kelly Gooden, Peggy W. Hambright, Geri Harris, Judy Henline, Paula Holdren, Elizabeth H. Lindsay, Debra Liverman, Thad McLaurin, Christa New, Janet Radcliffe, Karen Richmond, Marsha Schmus, Irene Taylor, Christine A. Thuman, Patricia Twohey, Stephanie Willett-Smith, Maureen Winkler
Copy Editors: Sylvan Allen, Lynn Bemer Coble, Karen Brewer Grossman, Karen L. Huffman, Amy Kirtley-Hill, Jennifer Rudisill, Debbie Shoffner, Gina Sutphin
Cover Artists: Clevell Harris, Clint Moore
Art Coordinator: Theresa Lewis Goode
Artists: Jennifer Tipton Bennett, Cathy Spangler Bruce, Pam Crane, Teresa Davidson, Nick Greenwood, Clevell Harris, Ivy L. Koonce, Shelia Krill, Rob Mayworth, Nancee McClure, Clint Moore, Becky J. Radtke, Greg D. Rieves, Rebecca Saunders, Barry Slate, Donna K. Teal
Typesetters: Lynette Dickerson, David Jarrell, Mark Rainey
Indexer: Elizabeth Findley Caran
The Mailbox® Books.com: Kimberley Bruck (manager); Debra Liverman, Sharon Murphy (associate editors); Jennifer L. Tipton (designer/artist); Troy Lawrence, Stuart Smith (production artists); Karen White (editorial assistant); Paul Fleetwood, Xiaoyun Wu (systems)

President, The Mailbox Book Company™: Joseph C. Bucci
Director of Book Planning and Development: Chris Poindexter
Book Development Managers: Elizabeth H. Lindsay, Thad McLaurin, Susan Walker
Curriculum Director: Karen P. Shelton
Traffic Manager: Lisa K. Pitts
Librarian: Dorothy C. McKinney
Editorial and Freelance Management: Karen A. Brudnak
Editorial Training: Irving P. Crump
Editorial Assistants: Terrie Head, Hope Rodgers, Jan E. Witcher

©2002, 1996 by THE EDUCATION CENTER, INC.
All rights reserved.
ISBN #1-56234-144-8

Except as provided for herein, no part of this publication may be reproduced or transmitted in any form or by any means, electronic or mechanical, including photocopying, recording, or storing in any information storage and retrieval system or electronic online bulletin board, without prior written permission from The Education Center, Inc. Permission is given to the original purchaser to reproduce patterns and reproducibles for individual classroom use only and not for resale or distribution. Reproduction for an entire school or school system is prohibited. Please direct written inquiries to TheEducation Center, Inc., P.O. Box 9753, Greensboro, NC 27429-0753. The Education Center®, The Mailbox®, the mailbox/post/grass logo, and The Mailbox Book Company™ are trademarks of The Education Center, Inc., and may be the subject of one or more federal trademark registrations. All other brand or product names are trademarks or registered trademarks of their respective companies.

Manufactured in the United States
10 9 8 7 6 5 4 3 2 1

MARCH
Table of Contents

Online Extras 1

About This Book 2

March Planner Pages 4
  Be prepared for a great month with these handy reproducibles:
  • teacher's resource list of March's special days
  • reproducible calendar of free-time activities for students
  • reproducible award and a student desktag

Spring 8
  These cheery, skill-based activities are just the lifeline you need to chase away those winter blues.

American Women 18
  Celebrate National Women's History Month with these star-spangled ideas.

Measurement Skills 30
  Pump your students up with this hefty collection of measurement activities.

St. Patrick's Day 44
  Dip into this pot of golden ideas for celebrating St. Patrick's Day.

Ireland 54
  Don't forget to pack these great cross-curricular activities when you travel to Ireland—the land of mist, magic, and mystique.

Plants 62
  These skill-based ideas will get your students digging into the power of plants.

Eggs 76
  Crack open these "eggs-cellent" Grade A activities.

Nutrition 84
  Serve up these healthful ideas to celebrate National Nutrition Month®.

Answer Keys 92

Index 94

March Calendar

Newspaper in Education Week

Celebrated the first full week in March, this program promotes the use of newspapers in the classroom. Have students scan a newspaper, identifying the various parts and their contents. Ask students what information they would like to see in the paper, such as new toy reviews, suggestions for "great escapes" for kids, or tips on kids' fashions. Have each student choose one of the topics on which to write a news article.

National Procrastination Week

During the first week in March join the many people across the country who celebrate "putting off till tomorrow everything that needn't be done today." Share with students the meaning of the word *procrastination* and the many ways in which we all procrastinate. Have each student pledge in writing to perform a chore or task for a busy family member or friend so that she may indulge in a "wee bit o' procrastination."

American Red Cross Month

The Red Cross, founded in Switzerland in 1863, consists of over ten million volunteers dedicated to relieving human suffering. It provides services to armed forces, veterans, and youths, as well as relief during such disasters as floods, droughts, fires, tornadoes, and hurricanes. Ask students if they've ever experienced one of these disasters. Assign each group of students one disaster to research. Have each group devise an emergency plan for dealing with its disaster.

3—Birthday of Alexander Graham Bell

Alexander Graham Bell was born on this day in 1847 in Edinburgh, Scotland. He helped his father educate the hearing impaired. In his spare time, he discovered how to send messages of electric speech. This led to his patent of the first telephone in 1876. Ask students, "If you could call anyone in the world, who would it be?" Have each student write a brief paragraph telling who he would call and the questions he would ask during the call.

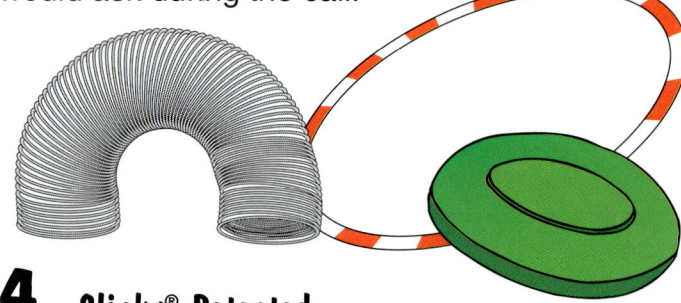

4—Slinky® Patented

On this day in 1947, Richard and Betty James received a patent for an unusual toy called the *Slinky®*. Its thin, coiled wire allowed it to "walk" down stairs. After being displayed in a major department store, all of the 400 Slinky® toys for sale sold out in 90 minutes. Invite students to imagine themselves as inventors of a new toy. What would the toy look like? How would it operate? Who would use the toy, and where would it be used? What would it be called? Have each student write and illustrate a description of her new invention.

6—Birth of Michelangelo

Michelangelo was born on this day in 1475 in Caprese, Italy. This renowned Renaissance painter, sculptor, architect, and poet had a profound influence on Western art. His works include the sculptures of *David* and *The Pieta,* and the painted ceiling of the Sistine Chapel at the Vatican in Rome. As part of March's Youth Art Month, have students illustrate replicas of their favorite masterpieces or create their own works of art.

12—Anniversary of the Death of Anne Frank

On March 12, 1945, 15-year-old Anne Frank died at a concentration camp called Bergen-Belsen. She and her family had been hiding with others in the annex behind her father's business for over two years during World War II. Anne kept a diary of her days spent in the annex. Her diary was published in 1947. Discuss with students what life would be like if they had to hide with their families in an annex. Have them list ten items that they would need most during such a time of hiding.

13—Planet Uranus Is Discovered

On this day in 1781, Uranus was discovered by an English astronomer named Sir William Herschel. Uranus is the seventh planet from the sun (about 1,786,400,000 miles). It is 31,763 miles in diameter, its temperature is –357°F, and its rotation is 17 hours and 8 minutes. Have students identify the digit that is common to all of these numbers *(7)*. Challenge each student to find seven more facts about the planet to share with her classmates.

31—Daylight Saving Time

On this day in 1918, people first moved their clocks ahead one hour to conserve power and provide more usable daylight hours in the afternoon and early evening. In the United States, daylight saving time begins on the first Sunday in April and ends on the last Sunday in October. Have students explain how we save money, people, resources, and energy during daylight saving time.

FREE-TIME FUN for March!

Tackle these 20 terrific tasks when you finish your work.

Monday	Tuesday	Wednesday	Thursday	Friday
March 3 is "I want you to be happy" day. Think of a person whom you would like to make happy; then do something nice for him or her.	National Pig Day is celebrated annually in March. The pig is considered an intelligent animal. If a pig were substitute-teaching in your class, what would you learn that day?	Ireland is often called the Emerald Isle because it's a land of beautiful green countryside. List other names for the color green.	Count the number of students wearing green today. Make a pie graph to show your findings.	A clover belongs to the group of plants called *trifolium* because it has three leaves. List other words that have the letters *tri* in them.
March is National Nutrition Month®. Make up a school lunch menu for each day of the week. Be sure to include each of the four food groups in each day's menu.	The Irish are known for their potatoes. List as many recipes as you can that use potatoes as an ingredient.	Books are often categorized by title or author. What other ways could you categorize the books in your classroom library?	How are the desks arranged in your classroom? Illustrate a new seating arrangement.	March 14 is Save a Spider Day. List eight places that a spider could be found.
St. Patrick's Day is March 17. Describe what a holiday would be like if it were named after you.	March's wind makes it a great month to fly kites. Draw a new design for a kite.	Straw Hat Week is celebrated each March about two weeks before Easter. Draw a straw hat decorated with some of the things a teacher or other professional could use in the workplace.	The Irish Sea is a body of water between Ireland and England. Name three other seas and tell where they are located.	Memory Day is celebrated on March 21. Many numbers, such as phone numbers, need to be memorized. List other numbers that you are encouraged to memorize. My phone number is 555-0000.
Many things come in pairs. List as many items as you can that come in pairs.	Four-leaf clovers are supposed to bring good luck. Describe an item that you think is lucky, and tell why.	March 26 is the poet Robert Frost's birthday. Write a poem for a friend. *Stopping by the Woods on a Snowy Evening By Robert Frost*	March 29 is Teacher Appreciation Day. Write a letter to your teacher telling why you appreciate her.	March is said to "come in like a lion and go out like a lamb." Tell what you think this means. Does this expression fit March's weather this year?

Note to the teacher: Have each student staple a copy of this page inside a file folder. Direct students to store their completed work inside their folders.

Patterns

Desktag: Make copies for students on construction paper. Have each student personalize and decorate his pattern; then laminate the patterns and use them as desktags during March.

Award: Make multiple copies. Keep them handy at your desk during the month of March. When a student earns an award, write her name on the appropriate line. Allow the student to color and cut out the bottom ticket to use anytime during the month for a special treat, such as candy, free time, or a homework pass.

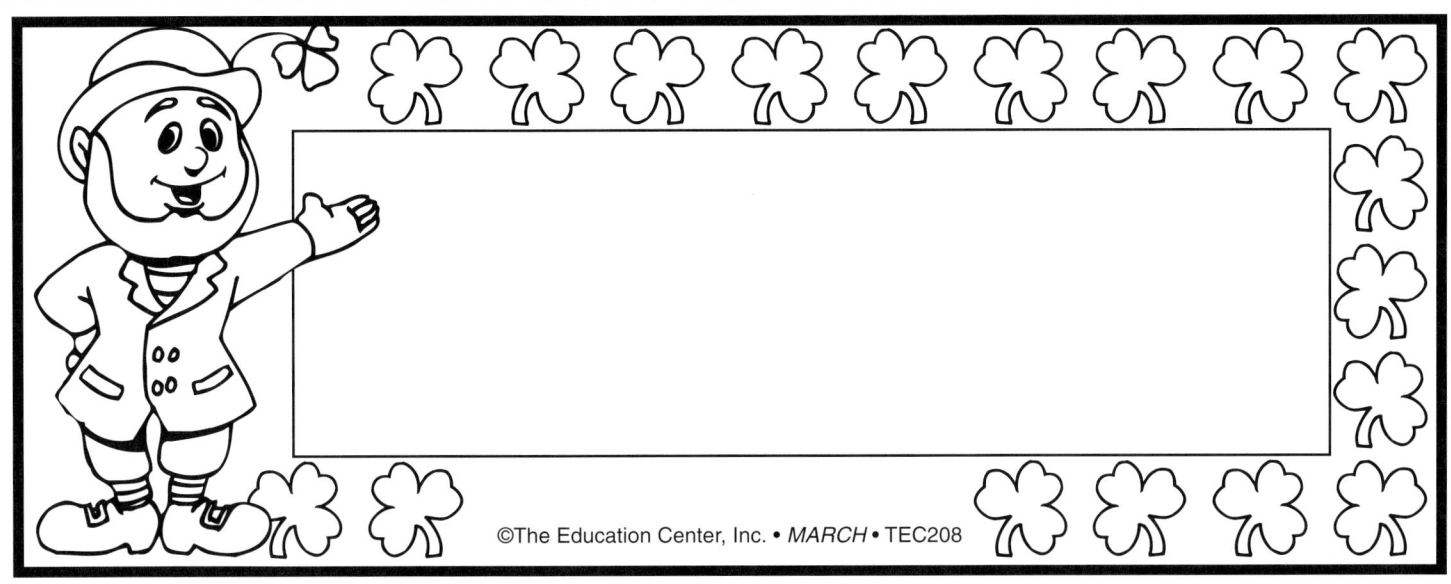

Saved by Spring!

Spring—each year we wait in anticipation for the season. Arriving just in time for you to say good-bye to winter and hello to spring, these creative activities will bring a breath of fresh air into your classroom!

by Paula Holdren and Elizabeth H. Lindsay

Lifesavers
Identifying evidence of seasonal changes, making a personal connection

Just when the winter blahs threaten to overtake you, Mother Nature throws you a lifeline on the gentle breeze of spring. With this breeze come signs of new life, such as the blooming of flowers, the buzzing of insects, and the birth of baby animals. With the help of your students, list these and other "lifesaving" signs on the board.

Bring these signs of spring into your classroom by having each of your students create a spring lifesaving ring. Distribute a 9" x 12" sheet of white paper to each child, instructing her to draw and cut out an eight-inch circle. Next, have the student draw and cut out a three-inch hole from the center of the circle. Direct her to label the ring "SS Spring." Finally, on the ring, have her write her favorite spring lifesavers and tell why they are her favorites.

Share the lifesavers by creating a nautical bulletin board using the "SS Spring" ship pattern on page 14. Attach the rings to the boat with string, and sail happily into spring!

Welcome, Spring!
Motivating students

Put out the welcome mat for the new season and usher spring right through your door with these quick suggestions!

1. Invest in a brightly colored stamp pad and a new "spring-y" rubber stamp to add some pizzazz to your comments on assignments.
2. Keep a pot of tulips or a bouquet of daffodils on your desk.
3. Scan local garage sales for a large jigsaw puzzle with a spring scene (or ask for a donation). Set it up in the corner of your room for free-time fun.
4. Encourage your students to eat lunch with someone they normally don't eat with. It's never too late to make a friend!
5. A fresh face can add zip to a tired routine. Swap classes with a colleague for a story, a lesson, a period, or even a day. Teachers and students will feel refreshed when the exchange is over!
6. Take a break on a breezy afternoon. Hold a paper airplane contest or fly colorful kites.
7. Bring in an inflatable child's pool and a couple of lawn chairs to add atmosphere to your reading corner. Add some "hot" new books to get the reading habit sizzling by summer!
8. Spring has traditionally been the season to clean up. Give your classroom a face-lift by breaking out the cloths and buckets. Have students clean out their desks; then send them on a mission around the room to dust, straighten, and sweep. In no time, your room will be dazzling!
9. With spring comes new life. What better way to have your students experience this than by bringing it right to your classroom? Invite a trained volunteer from a local SPCA or Humane Society to share some young, furry friends with your class. Your students will enjoy the hands-on experience and learn something about the organization.
10. Help a fine-feathered friend build a new spring home. Birds need lots of materials to build their nests. Collect short bits of yarn, dryer lint, cotton, and hair. Place the materials in a small basket. Hang the basket from a tree and before you know it, you'll have the birds coming from all around to collect the scraps.

The Verdict Is In...
Identifying evidence of seasonal changes, researching seasonal changes

March means spring is here; or does it? In some parts of the country, this month can still mean lots of blustery, rainy weather. Even though the calendar says that it's March, we may feel that spring will never arrive! Give your students' spirits a boost by challenging them to track down signs of spring by using their senses—sight, sound, smell, and touch. First, have your class brainstorm the many signs of spring. Then put students in pairs and duplicate the pattern on page 14 for each pair. If it's a nice day, venture outside and allow your springtime sleuths to look for evidence of one of these signs and record it on the report. Next, have each pair research to explain why or how the sign occurs and write the proof on the report. For example, "The air is warmer because this part of Earth is now closer to the sun." Share group findings and show off their sleuthing by displaying the reports on the door or in the hallway. Caption their efforts "The Verdict Is In…Spring Is Here!"

How to Celebrate Spring
Explanatory writing

Looking for some refreshing writing ideas? Watch your students' explanatory writing blossom as they spring into these seasonal how-to paragraphs. Have each student compose a paragraph on one of the topics below. For a colorful display, have each student copy her edited paragraph onto flower-shaped notepaper. Then have the student create a cover by tracing the flower shape onto a large piece of floral wallpaper, and cutting it out. Staple each covered paragraph to the board; then add green stems, leaves, and grass, as well as a white picket fence. Title the display "A Garden of Writing Delights!"

- How to chase away winter
- How to welcome spring
- How to jump into a water puddle
- How to store winter clothes
- How to pick flowers
- How to fly a kite
- How to hit a baseball
- How to ride a bike
- How to play hopscotch
- How to daydream
- How to blow bubbles
- How to catch a frog

Spring Friendship Baskets
Building character through a community project

The holidays are long gone, and so are many people's commitments to those who are less fortunate. Bring a little joy to this season by donating baskets of spring goodies to a homeless shelter or to a family down on its luck. Provide each small group of students with a box, colorful sheets of bulletin board paper, tape, and markers. Direct each group to cover its box with the paper and make a decorative paper handle. Have each group decorate its box with colorful spring themes and messages of goodwill and friendship.

Call a local YMCA, Jewish (or Catholic or Lutheran) Family Services, Big Brothers/Big Sisters, or the American Red Cross. Find out what items are needed, such as food and clothing items, household supplies, and school supplies. If you are helping a residential home, ask if you may provide drinks, sandwiches, and seasonal cupcakes or cookies along with student-made cards or placemats. To fill the baskets, have your students write notes to families and friends requesting the items, or enlist the aid of colleagues and community members through the school bulletin board or newsletter. After the donations are collected and the items are delivered, you and your students will feel uplifted while others will benefit from your caring thoughts.

Spectacular Spring Swap
Motivating students to read, building character through a community project

As an old saying goes, "One man's trash is another man's treasure." Exploit the urge for spring cleaning by holding a special book swap. Ask students (with parental permission, of course!) to search their desks, closets, bookcases, and any other place these treasures may be lurking for one to three books that they would each like to donate to the swap.

Make a class supply of the ticket pattern on page 14. Give each student one ticket for each book brought in. Be sure that students understand that they will not get back the books they donate. When all donations are in, set up an attractive display. Invite each student to trade in his tickets—one for each "new" book. Take the sharing one step further by encouraging each student to donate at least one of his selections to the classroom library or a charitable organization. Let the excitement of new books start your students reading throughout the season!

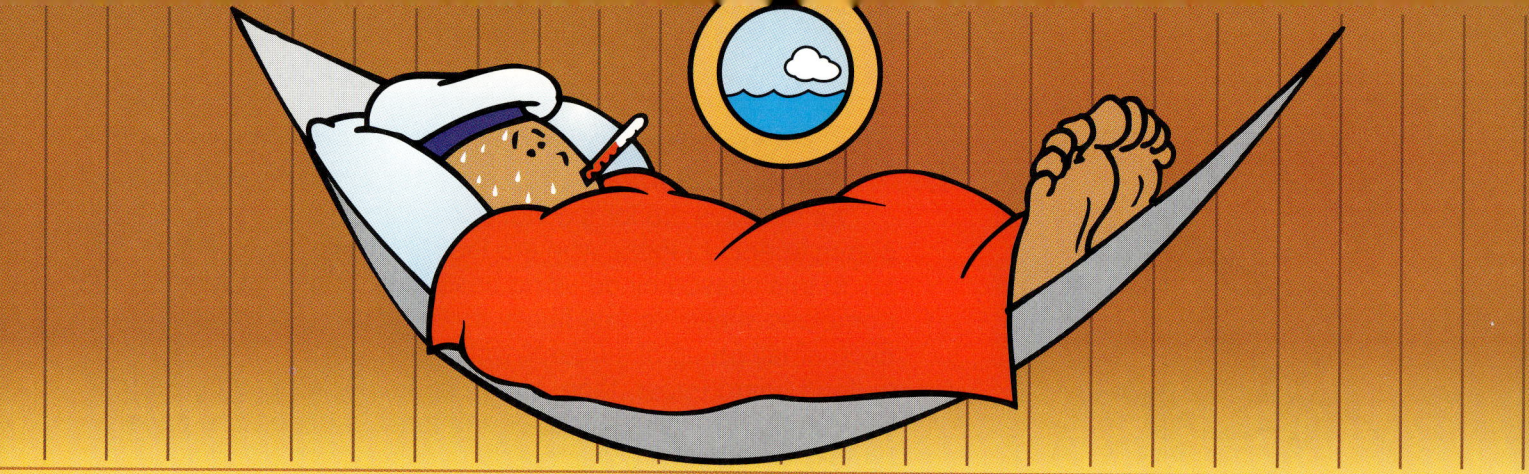

Rx for a Weak Vocabulary
Building vocabulary, writing for a purpose

The weather's warming up and the symptoms are clear. Your students have caught the "talking bug." Instead of trying to cure this disease, spread it! Pass out dictionaries and ask each student to select ten words that he feels no one else will be able to define. Direct him to write each word on his paper. Next to each word, have him write two definitions: one real and one phony. Pair each child with a partner, and have students in each pair exchange papers. A student earns one point for each word his partner incorrectly defines. When the pairs have finished, ask each student to choose five of his favorite vocabulary words. Challenge him to incorporate any of the five words into a written assignment or class discussion during the week. Every word that is used correctly earns him one bonus point. This will prove to be a quick-and-easy treatment for such a widespread disease!

And Then There Was...Spring
Understanding seasonal changes, creative writing

Four times a year, we experience a change of seasons. Each season lasts about three months, because it takes the earth this long—12 months—to travel around the sun. As it travels, different parts of the earth are closer to the sun, which affects the amount of light and heat each part receives. The first day of spring is called the spring equinox. (In the Northern Hemisphere, spring begins about March 21.) At this time, the sun is directly opposite the earth's equator and there are the same number of daytime and nighttime hours. In ancient times people celebrated this day because it signaled the beginning of the growing season.

The ancients did not have a scientific explanation for what caused the change of seasons. So to explain these mysterious events in nature, they created stories. The Greek myth of Demeter and Persephone is one such example. Obtain a copy of this myth or a book of Greek mythology from your school librarian. After sharing the myth with your students, ask the following questions: Does the story offer reasonable explanations for the changing of the seasons? What specific examples are given for changes such as temperature, length of daytime, budding of trees, and growing of plants?

Next, have each student write and illustrate a modern myth to explain why we have the seasons. Instruct each student to pay special attention to character, setting, and explanation of events. Display the stories for all to enjoy.

Written in the Wind
Writing poetry

March blows in National Poetry Month and the birthdate of American poet Robert Frost (March 26, 1874). Since weather is often a theme in poetry, what better topic to write about than March's winds? Challenge your students to brainstorm windy words and phrases. A sample list is shown below. Create a master list for all to use. Encourage each student to incorporate these windy expressions in a haiku, diamante, cinquain, free-verse, or concrete poem. You'll be in for a windfall of wondrous writing!

- wind
- windbag
- wind-bell
- windblast
- windblown
- wind-borne
- windbreak
- windburn
- windchill
- wind chime
- windfall
- windmill
- windpipe
- windsock
- windstorm
- windswept
- wind tunnel
- windward
- windy

- An ill wind that bloweth no man to good
- Awake, O north wind
- Blow, blow, thou winter wind
- blowin' in the wind
- blust'ring wind
- Come wind, come weather
- fly upon the wings of the wind
- friends who go with the wind
- gone with the wind
- hear the wind blow
- how the wind blows
- impatient as the wind
- inherit the wind
- like Wind I go
- take the wind out of one's sails
- throw caution to the wind
- Unhelped by any wind
- With hey, ho, the wind and the rain
- written in wind

The Beginning of the End
Reflecting on goals and objectives

With spring comes the final phase of the school year in most parts of the country. This is a good time to pause and reflect on what has been accomplished and to refocus goals and objectives in order to end the year on a positive note.

To help your students do this, copy the SOS reproducible on page 15 for each of them to complete. Tell each student to fill it out honestly because it will help you make plans for the rest of this year, as well as plan for next year. After the forms have been collected and analyzed, you and your students will breeze happily toward a positive and productive end of school!

Patterns
Use the ticket with "Spectacular Spring Swap" on page 11. Use the report with "The Verdict Is In…" on page 10.

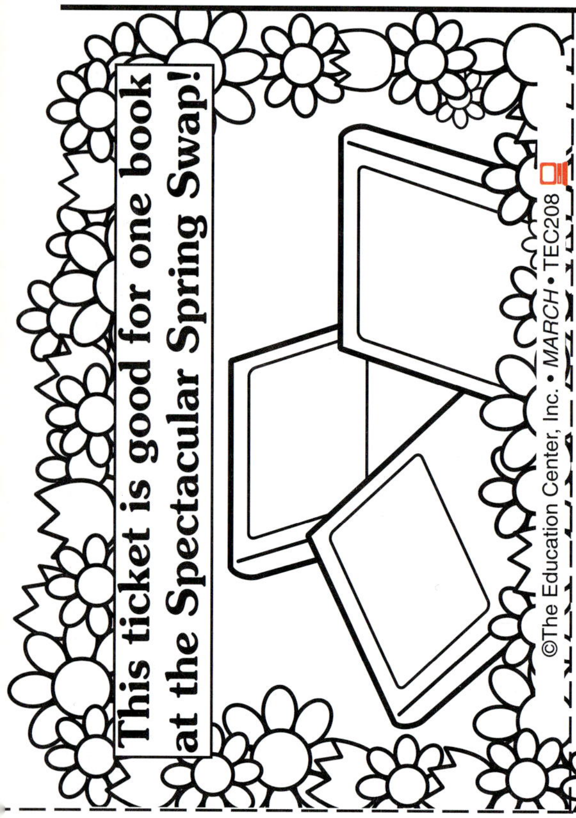

This ticket is good for one book at the Spectacular Spring Swap!

Names _____ Date _____

Springtime Sleuth Report

Evidence observed: _____
_____
_____
_____

Proof: _____
_____
_____
_____

Verdict: Spring is here!

©The Education Center, Inc. • MARCH • TEC208

Pattern
Enlarge and use the pattern with "Lifesavers" on page 8.

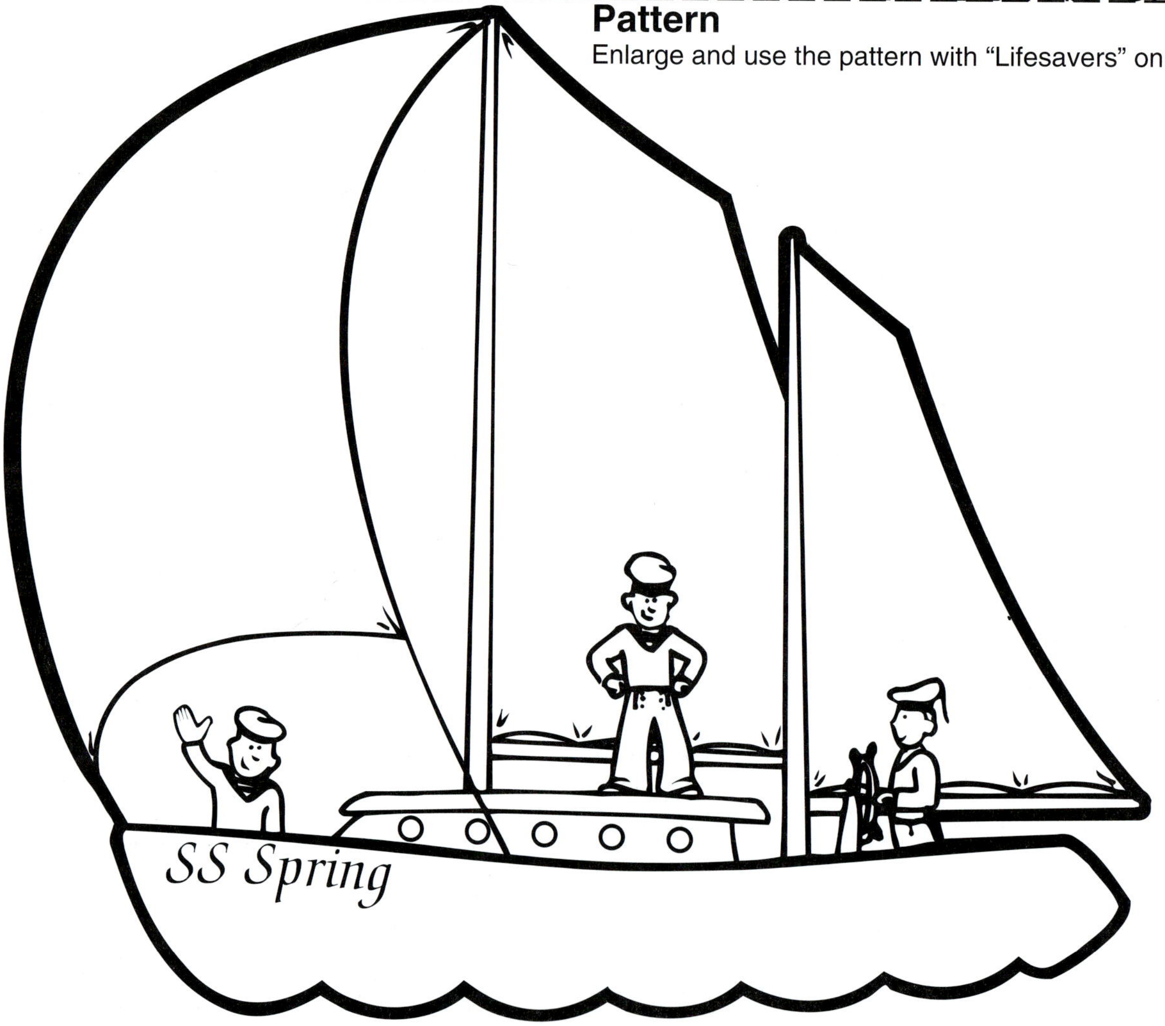

SS Spring

©The Education Center, Inc. • MARCH • TEC208

Name_____ *Student survey*

Spring On Suggestions (SOS)!

Spring is here, which means we've come a long way since the beginning of the school year. Please take a few minutes to answer the survey below. Your honest answers will help me map out the rest of our year and ensure that it is "springing with success!"

SOS

1. The best thing about school so far this year is _____.
2. The worst thing about school so far this year is _____.
3. My favorite subject is _____ because _____
   _____.
4. My least favorite subject is _____ because _____
   _____.
5. I'm still fuzzy about _____. I think it's because _____
   _____.
6. I want to learn about _____.
7. Could you please read _____?
8. I wish I didn't have to _____.
9. I don't think you know _____.
10. We don't spend enough time _____.
11. We spend too much time _____.
12. If I could change two things about class, they would be _____
    _____.
13. I can _____ to help you and the class.
14. I learn best when _____.
15. I feel good about _____.

Bonus Box: If you could trade places with your teacher on a spring day, what would you teach the class? Plan a lesson for the day.

©The Education Center, Inc. • *MARCH* • TEC208

Note to the teacher: Use with "The Beginning of the End" on page 13.

Name_____ _Seasonal contract_

Sailing Into Spring

Explore a new world—spring! Complete _____ of the following activities by _____ and sail happily into spring!

1. Name three things you think of when you hear the word *spring*. Draw a picture of one of your thoughts.

2. What kinds of weather occur during spring? Research one type of weather that occurs in spring and explain it in a paragraph.

3. What colors do you think of during spring? Research why we see the colors in a rainbow. List your findings on a colorful sheet of construction paper.

4. What three feelings does spring bring to your mind? Express your feelings in a poem about spring.

5. Which foods are available mainly during spring? Prepare a spring dinner menu for your family. Include the main meal, a drink, and a dessert.

6. What are your favorite articles of spring clothing? Design a T-shirt that celebrates spring.

7. What sports are played during spring? Using an index card, create a sports card. On the front of the card, draw a picture of the game being played. On the back of the card, list the important facts about the game: the object of the game, rules, equipment, and players.

8. What animals do you see in the springtime? Research an animal that comes out of hibernation during this time of year. Describe its springtime behaviors in a paragraph.

9. What types of plants do you see growing or blooming during the spring? Draw and label a design for a backyard garden that includes some of your favorite plants and flowers.

10. Which bugs bother you most during the spring? Write an original story about a bothersome bug.

11. What are some of the springtime activities that you enjoy most? Create a party invitation that includes a schedule of your favorite activities.

12. What kinds of things might need to be cleaned during the spring? List as many things as you can think of that need to be cleaned at your house.

©The Education Center, Inc. • MARCH • TEC208

Note to the teacher: Make one copy of this page; then write the required number of activities and the due date on the blanks before duplicating one for each student. Have each student staple his copy inside a folder; then have him store his work inside the folder.

Name _____

Problem solving

Spring "Sale-ebration"!

Zack's Sport Shack is having a giant sale on this season's hottest items—everything is priced to go! Solve the problem on each shopping bag. Write the answer on the blank.

Price tags:
- All-Star Baseballs — $5.95 each
- Kinkless Kite String — $2.58 for two packages
- Goofless Golf Balls — $7.20 for a box of 12
- Major League Baseball Caps — $6.98 each
- Fearless Flashlights — $3.45 each
- Speedy Skateboards — $15.25 each
- Flying Streak Track Shoes — $27.75 pair
- Great Catch Fishing Rods — $18.50 each
- Super Shot Squirt Guns — $4.20 each
- Blazer Bicycles — $55.00 each
- Championship Rollerblades — $44.40 pair
- Hoopla Hula-Hoops — $3.99 each

Problems:

1. It's the start of the season. Your team needs twelve baseballs. What's the cost?

2. You only need one package of kite string. How much do you spend?

3. The box of golf balls is missing three. You only pay for the nine left. How much do you pay?

4. What a steal! Buy four of the baseball caps. What's the total price?

5. One flashlight needs two batteries. The batteries cost $0.82 each. What's your total for all three items?

6. You give Zack $20.00 for the skateboard. What's your change?

7. You buy two pairs of track shoes. What combination of bills do you need to give Zack? What change will you get back?

8. The reel is missing from the fishing rod. Zack will take $8.65 off the price. What will be the new price?

9. Your mom gave you $10.00. How many squirt guns can you buy?

10. If you buy two bikes, Zack will give you 10% off each one. How much will each bike then cost?

11. If you buy one pair of Rollerblades, Zack will give you 30% off. How much will you save?

12. Hula-Hoops are "Buy one, get one free." You need ten for your party. How much will you spend?

Bonus Box: You've been hired to advertise Zack's Spring "Sale-ebration." On the back of this paper, detail your plans to promote the sale and bring in hundreds of customers!

Saluting the Ladies!
Star-Spangled Suggestions for Teaching About Famous American Women

March is National Women's History Month. Participate with these star-studded activities honoring the women who have inspired our country from sea to shining sea.

by Patricia Twohey

Women Worth Remembering
Recognizing contributions of others, making a personal connection

Part One: Ignite interest about famous American women with this simple investigation. Ask each student to write the names of five famous American women who have contributed to our society. Then instruct the student to write a sentence next to each name that tells why he selected that woman. Collect the students' papers, keeping them until the end of the unit.

Part Two: To culminate the unit, return the papers collected in Part One. Have students discuss whether they would change any of their choices and why. Then give each student a 12" x 18" sheet of white paper. Instruct the student to divide the sheet into six 6-inch squares using a marker. Direct the student to choose five women whom he has learned about in the unit and write the name of each woman in a different square. In the sixth and remaining square, have him write the name of a woman he knows personally who has been important to him. Distribute crayons so that the student can illustrate each square, with an event from each woman's life as shown. Assess each student's learning by having him explain his artwork to the class.

Famous First Ladies
Researching famous American women

Many outstanding women have served as first ladies of our country while their husbands were president. Challenge your students to a scavenger hunt to acquaint them with some of the women who have worked alongside their husbands to make our country great. Give each team of two or three students a copy of the reproducible on page 24 and ample resources for conducting the search. After the hunt, take time to discuss each first lady's contribution.

To obtain resources and additional information, contact the National Women's History Project (an educational nonprofit organization), 7738 Bell Road, Windsor, CA 95492 or call (707) 838-6000.

Martha Washington

Notable Singers
Recognizing contributions of others, researching famous American women

Create a melodious bulletin board from notes that feature American female singers. On light-colored paper, make two copies of the musical-note pattern on page 25 for each student. Next, print each name from the list below on the stem of a different music note. Give each student a programmed note plus a blank note pattern. Instruct the student to use reference materials to find and fill in the information about the singer on the programmed note. Then direct the student to repeat the assignment using the blank note pattern to feature his favorite contemporary female singer.

Meanwhile, cut one treble clef symbol and one bass clef symbol from black paper. Staple the clefs to the left edge of the bulletin board as shown. Then make a musical staff by stapling five horizontal rows of black yarn from each clef to the right edge of the board as shown. Pin the students' completed notes to the bulletin board. If desired, encourage students to bring in cassette tapes or compact discs of these recording artists to share with the class!

Extend the life of the board by updating it as each new category of women is studied. Just change the title and duplicate additional music-note patterns after whiting-out and reprogramming the original one.

American Female Singers

Marian Anderson	Carole King
Joan Baez	Barbara Mandrell
Maria Callas	Reba McEntire
Mariah Carey	Bette Midler
Judy Collins	Rosa Ponselle
Ella Fitzgerald	Leontyne Price
Aretha Franklin	Beverly Sills
Billie Holiday	Bessie Smith
Lena Horne	Barbra Streisand
Whitney Houston	Tina Turner
Mahalia Jackson	

Marian Anderson

You've Come a Long Way, Ladies!
Acknowledging contributions in history, researching famous American women

Honor the women who have blazed the trail to women's rights by creating a class timeline. Gather encyclopedias, biographies, and other resources related to women's rights. Copy the timeline form on page 25 for each student. Write each name listed below on a separate slip of paper. Have each student draw one name. Direct the student to research and complete a timeline form about that woman. If a student finishes early, have him complete a timeline form for one or more of the dates listed on the historical background chart below. Stretch a string from one corner of the classroom to another. Attach the completed forms to the string in chronological order. Have students examine the completed timeline, noting any patterns or trends in this visual history of women's rights.

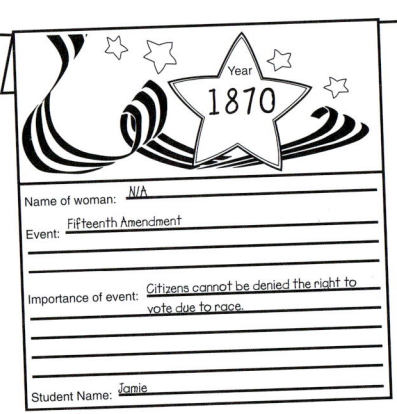
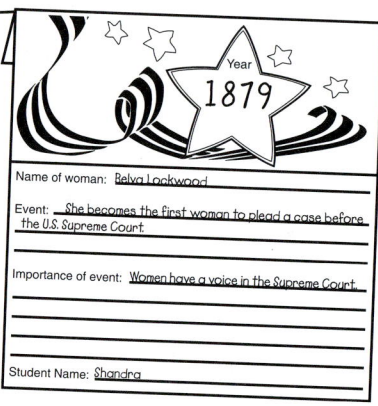
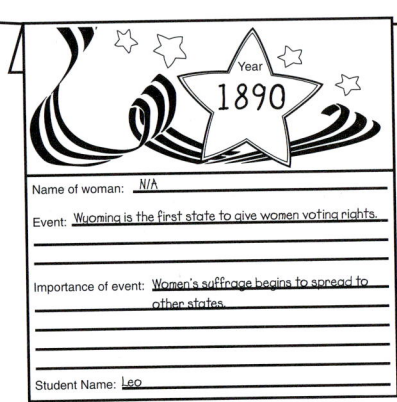

Women Who Worked for Women's Rights

Bella Abzug	Shirley Chisholm	Patsy Mink	Janet Reno
Mary Anderson	Geraldine Ferraro	Carol Moseley-Braun	Margaret Chase Smith
Susan B. Anthony	Betty Friedan	Lucretia Mott	Elizabeth Cady Stanton
Amelia Jenks Bloomer	Ruth Bader Ginsburg	Sandra Day O'Connor	Gloria Steinem
Hattie Wyatt Caraway	Belva Lockwood	Frances Perkins	Lucy Stone
Carrie Chapman Catt	Clare Boothe Luce	Jeannette Rankin	Naomi Wolf

Historical Background

- **1830** All white males can vote.
- **1870** Citizens cannot be denied the right to vote due to race (Fifteenth Amendment).
- **1890** Wyoming is the first state to give women voting rights.
- **1920** All citizens can vote regardless of sex (Nineteenth Amendment).
- **1923** The Equal Rights Amendment is presented to Congress for the first time.
- **1964** The Civil Rights Act is extended to include women.
- **1972** Congress passes an Equal Rights Amendment and sends it to the states to be ratified.
- **1982** The Equal Rights Amendment fails (only 35 of the needed 38 states ratify it).

Sandra Day O'Connor

Training the Next Generation
Researching famous American women, writing for a purpose

How important have American women been to the development of education in the United States? Help students discover the answer to this question by dividing students into eight groups and assigning each group one educator from the chart below to feature on a poster. Direct each group to include the educator's name, date, and achievement on the poster, along with a likeness if possible.

Next, have each student write a letter to a female teacher who has made the greatest impact on his life. Direct the student to explain in the letter the reasons why this teacher was so special to him. As each student shares his letter, list the characteristics that he noted as being important in a good teacher. Finally, help each student find a way to deliver the letter to the teacher.

Year	Woman	Accomplishment in Education
Between 1805 & 1809	Elizabeth Ann Seton	Founder of the parochial (Catholic) school system in the United States.
1819	Emma Willard	Head of the first U.S. school to offer a college-level education for women.
1837	Mary Lyon	Head of Mount Holyoke Female Seminary (later Mount Holyoke College).
1860	Elizabeth P. Peabody	Founder of the first kindergarten in the United States.
1878	Kate Douglas Wiggin	Cofounder of the California Kindergarten Training School for teachers.
1882	Alice Freemen Palmer	President of Wellesley College (1882–1887).
1900	Mary Woolley	President of Mount Holyoke College (1900–1937).
1904	Mary McLeod Bethune	Founder of Daytona Normal and Industrial Institute for Negro Girls (now Bethune-Cookman College).

Designing Women
Understanding patterns and relationships among events, researching women's history

In 1851, Amelia Bloomer shocked society by wearing pants under her dress. Years later, in 1907, Annette Kellerman dared to appear on a Boston beach in a one-piece bathing suit and was immediately arrested. Amelia's "bloomers" and Kellerman's swimsuit are just two examples of how women's fashions have reflected their changing roles in society. Help students see this connection by creating a historical fashion display. Divide students into seven groups. Have each group investigate the fashions worn by women during one of the following time periods: the 1700s, the 1800s, the Roaring Twenties, World War II, the 1950s, the 1960s, and the present. Supply reference materials and have each group research the clothing styles of the period. In addition, have each group discover any attitudes or feelings toward women that were reflected in the types of clothes they were expected to wear.

Afterward, give each group an 8" x 5" piece of oaktag along with the art supplies it needs to make, decorate, and label a paper doll to represent its assigned time period. Have each group share its doll and its findings with the class. Hang each doll in its appropriate space on the class timeline constructed in "You've Come a Long Way, Ladies!"

Mary McLeod Bethune

Listening to the Heartbeat
Researching famous American women, writing poetry

American women poets have been listening to and recording the heartbeat of our nation since its earliest times. Challenge each student to select one poet from the list below. After reading several of her poems, have the student research additional facts and answer the following questions: What did this poet want to accomplish so that her life would not be in vain? What gave her life meaning? Read Emily Dickinson's poem to the class. Have each student use it to model her own poem about the poet she has researched. Display the completed poems on a bulletin board titled "Poetry: The Heartbeat of a Nation."

*If I can stop one heart from breaking,
I shall not live in vain:
If I can ease one life the aching,
Or cool one pain,
Or help one fainting robin
Unto his nest again,
I shall not live in vain.*
—Emily Dickinson

American Women Poets
Maya Angelou
Katharine Lee Bates
Anne Bradstreet
Gwendolyn Elizabeth Brooks
Emily Dickinson
Rita Dove
Emma Lazarus
Edna St. Vincent Millay
Marianne Moore
Mona Van Duyn
Phillis Wheatley

Cereal-Box Champions
Recognizing contributions of others, writing for a purpose

Seize the opportunity to publicize some extraordinary women athletes! Collect one cereal box for each pair of students. Have each pair cover its box with paper and then research one of the women athletes listed below. Instruct each pair to write a biographical sketch of the athlete and glue it to the back of the cereal box. Next, have the pair draw a picture of the athlete performing her sport and then glue it to the box's front. Instruct the partners to create a new name for the cereal in honor of the athlete it features. Display the completed boxes on a table in the media center next to the title "Breakfast of Champions!"

American Women Athletes
Bonnie Blair
Gertrude Ederle
Chris Evert
Peggy Fleming
Althea Gibson
Dorothy Hamill
Jackie Joyner-Kersee
Billie Jean King
Nancy Lopez
Wilma Rudolph
Helen Wills
Kristi Yamaguchi
Babe Didrikson Zaharias

Concentrating on Achievements
Acknowledging contributions in history

Celebrate National Women's History Month with a game that combines history and graphing skills. Duplicate and cut apart the 42 game cards on page 26. Cut 21 index cards in half; then paste a different game card onto each index-card half. Laminate the cards if desired. Next, pin colored yarn to a bulletin board to form a 6 x 7 grid as shown. Staple cut-out letters that spell the words WOMEN IN and HISTORY along the *x* and *y* axes as pictured. Shuffle the game cards and pin one card facedown to each of the grid's points.

To play the game, divide students into two teams. Have a Team A member call out two coordinate pairs of letters from the board, such as (W, R) and (IN, H). Instruct a Team B member to turn over the cards located at those intersecting points. Have this player also read the cards aloud and check to see if the letters in the corners of the cards match. If they do match, direct the student to remove the cards and give them to the player from Team A. Then award Team A two points and give Team B a turn at play. If the cards do not match, have the student turn the cards back over and proceed to give a Team B member a turn. End the game when all the cards have been matched. The team with the most points wins.

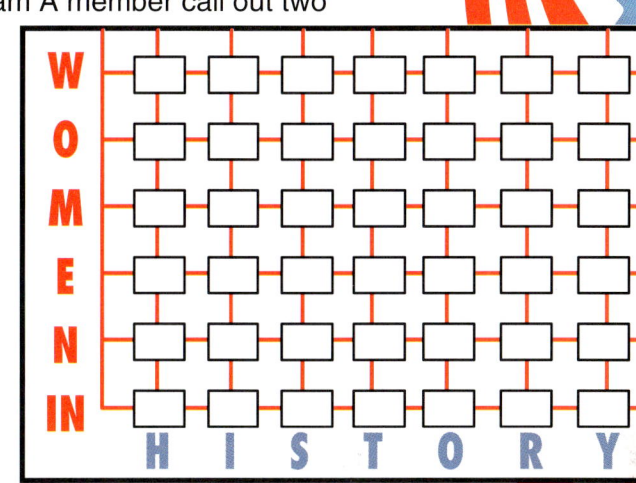

The "Write" Stuff!
Reading independently, responding to literature

Add a cooperative twist to your usual book-reporting format while studying American women. Divide students into teams of four. Display the list of American women authors below; then have each team select a different author. Give each team two to four weeks to read as many different books by this author as possible, with each team member reading a different book. At the end of the reading period, give each team a copy of the reproducible on page 27. Instruct each team to complete the activities on the reproducible and share its findings with the class. Repeat the activity as often as you like by having each team choose a different author each time.

American Women Authors for Children

Louisa May Alcott	Marguerite Henry
Judy Blume	Madeleine L'Engle
Frances Burnett	Lois Lenski
Betsy Byars	Lois Lowry
Ann Nolan Clark	Patricia MacLachlan
Beverly Cleary	Phyllis Reynolds Naylor
Elizabeth Coatsworth	Emily Neville
Marguerite de Angeli	Katherine Paterson
Elizabeth Enright	Cynthia Rylant
Eleanor Estes	Kate Seredy
Rachel Field	Elizabeth George Speare
Esther Forbes	Mildred D. Taylor
Paula Fox	Cynthia Voigt
Jean Craighead George	Laura Ingalls Wilder
Virginia Hamilton	Elizabeth Yates

Betsy Byars

Famous First Ladies Scavenger Hunt

Research skills

The wife of our country's president serves as first lady while her husband is in office. Every first lady works in her own way to serve our country. Help your group research the first ladies listed below. Then match each first lady with her accomplishment(s) by writing her initials inside the square of a clue box.

1. She was America's first first lady.	2. She redecorated the White House and made the mansion a historic tourist attraction.	3. She fought for equal rights for minority groups and worked with young people and the underprivileged.	4. She chaired the United Nation's Human Rights Commission and headed the Commission on the Status of Women.
5. She was a great-great-niece of Franklin Pierce, the 14th president of the United States.	6. She saved George Washington's portrait and many important government papers when the city of Washington was invaded by the British in 1814.	7. She supported women's rights and urged her husband to "remember the ladies" as new laws were proposed.	8. She was so popular that many women copied her hairstyle and fashions.
9. She wrote a daily newspaper column, many magazine articles, and several books.	10. She started the Foundation for Family Literacy and supported reading programs throughout the United States.	11. She was a distinguished lawyer and speaker who actively participated in her husband's presidency.	12. She was the first first lady to address the United Nations.
13. She shared her husband's battlefield hardships and even organized a sewing circle to mend soldiers' uniforms.	14. She wrote two books from her dogs' points of view and gave the money earned from them to charities.	15. She was the wife of the second president and the mother of the sixth president.	16. She helped write a low-cost health-care plan for her husband's administration on which Congress chose not to act.

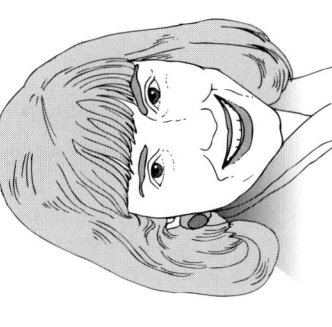

Abigail Adams
Hillary Rodham Clinton
Dolley Madison
Eleanor Roosevelt
Barbara Bush
Jacqueline Kennedy (Onassis)
Nancy Reagan
Martha Washington

©The Education Center, Inc. • *MARCH* • TEC208 • Key p. 92

Note to the teacher: Use with "Famous First Ladies" on page 18. Make one copy for each group. Supply reference materials such as encyclopedias, almanacs, and biographies. *America's Most Influential First Ladies* by Carl S. Anthony and *The Smithsonian Book of the First Ladies* are recommended as resources.

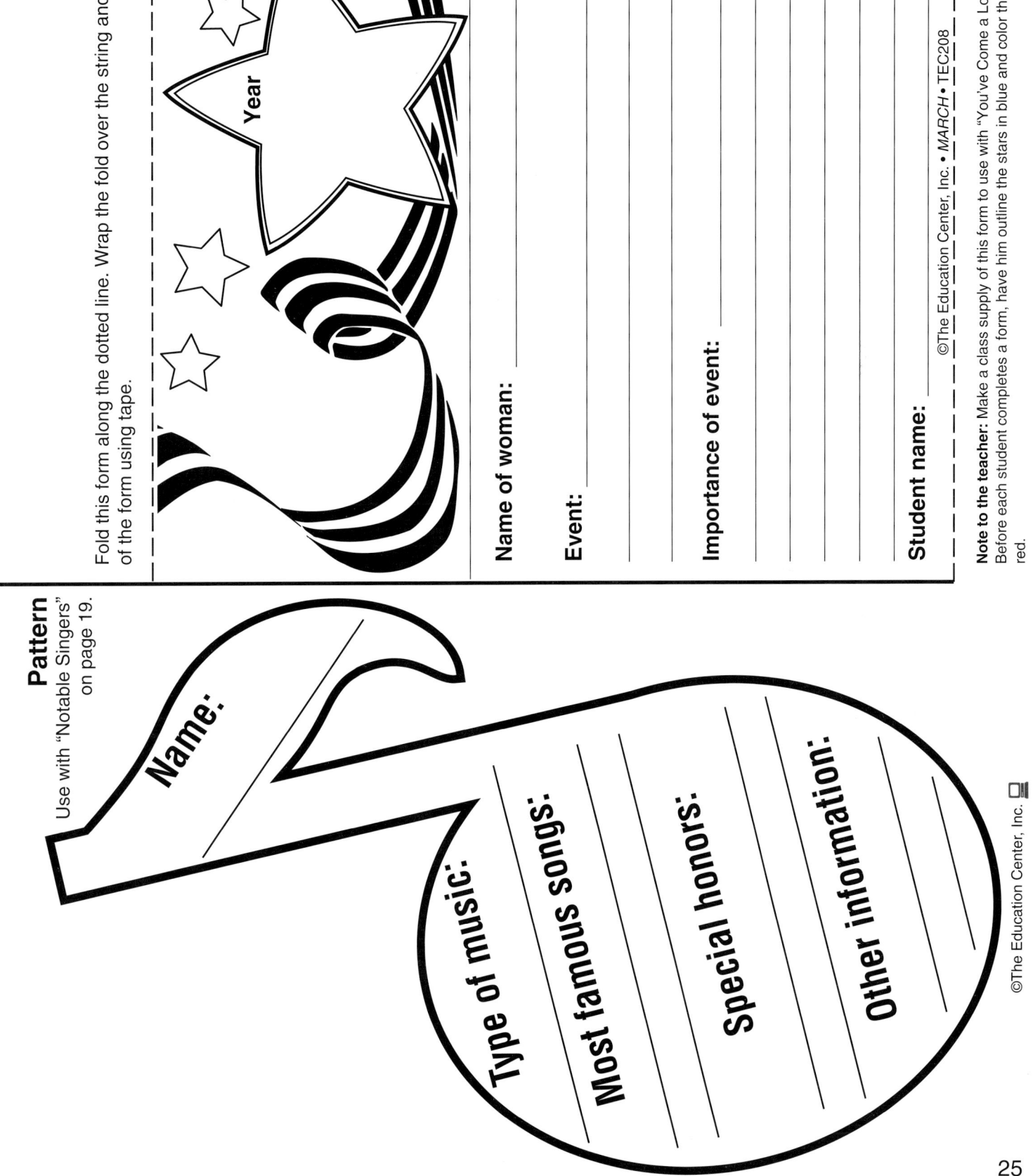

A Margaret Corbin	**A** This woman took her husband's place at his gun post after he was killed in a Revolutionary War battle in 1776.	**B** Rosa Parks	**B** This African-American woman's refusal to give up her bus seat to a white passenger led to the desegregation of the bus system in Montgomery, Alabama, in 1956.
C Pocahontas	**C** According to legend this Native American saved Captain John Smith from death in 1608.	**D** Betsy Ross	**D** This seamstress is believed to have sewn the first American flag in 1776.
E Harriet Tubman	**E** This former slave led about 300 slaves to freedom in Canada along the Underground Railroad.	**F** Lydia Darragh	**F** This woman saved American troops from disaster by warning General Washington about British battle plans.
G Esther Morris	**G** In 1870 this woman became the first woman justice of the peace in the United States.	**H** Sybil Ludington	**H** In 1777 this 16-year-old gathered together her father's regiment to fight the British at Danbury, Connecticut.
I Anne Hutchinson	**I** This religious reformer moved to Rhode Island after being banished from the Massachusetts Bay Colony in 1637.	**J** Clara Barton	**J** This woman gave supplies to wounded soldiers during the Civil War and later founded the American Red Cross.
K Dorothea Dix	**K** Through her activities hospitals for the insane and homeless were founded throughout the United States and Canada during the 1800s.	**L** Kateri Tekakwitha	**L** This seventeenth-century Native American was the first layperson to be recommended for sainthood in the Roman Catholic Church.
M Juliette Gordon Low	**M** This woman started the Girl Scouts of the United States of America in 1915.	**N** Sacagawea	**N** This Native American was the interpreter and guide for the Lewis and Clark expedition in 1805 and 1806.
O Sojourner Truth	**O** This former slave preached against slavery and for women's rights during the 1800s.	**P** Narcissa Whitman	**P** In 1836 she became the first white woman to cross the Rocky Mountains.
Q Jane Addams	**Q** This woman established the first settlement house, Hull House, in 1889 in Chicago. She won the Nobel Peace Prize in 1931.	**R** Julia Lathrop	**R** In 1899 this social worker set up the first juvenile court in the world. In 1912 she became the first chief of the U.S. Department of Labor's Children's Bureau.
S Molly Pitcher	**S** This woman carried water to thirsty soldiers during a Revolutionary War battle.	**T** Annie Oakley	**T** This famous markswoman performed with Buffalo Bill's Wild West Show from 1885 to 1902.
U Helen Keller	**U** Blind and deaf from the age of two, this woman became a famous speaker and writer during the early twentieth century.		

Team Members: _____   *Responding to literature*

The "Write" Stuff

Complete the information on this form together as a team and share your findings with the class.

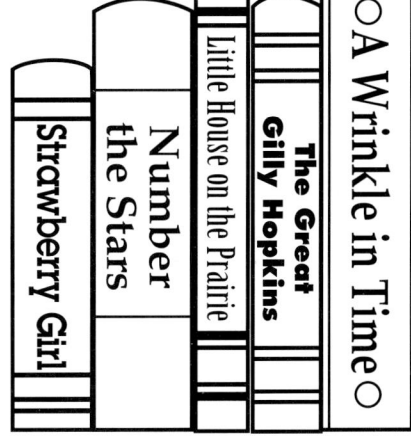

_____
Author's Name

A. Interesting facts about the author's life:	B. Titles of the books we read:

C. How the books were alike: (Type of literature, characters, setting, plot, theme, style)	D. How the books were different: (Type of literature, characters, setting, plot, theme, style)

E. What we liked about the books:	F. Why others should read the books:

©The Education Center, Inc. • *MARCH* • TEC208

Note to the teacher: Make one copy of this page for each group to use with "The 'Write' Stuff!" on page 23.

27

Name(s) _____ Due Date: _____ Contract: famous American women

Hats Off to the Ladies!

Color a hat each time you or your group completes an activity.

1. Many professional male athletes promote such products as athletic shoes and soft drinks. Pick a famous woman whom you have studied. Use her name and abilities to advertise a new product.

2. Write an eight- to ten-line poem about the woman from this unit whom you most admire.

3. Work with at least two other classmates to write and perform a skit about an important event from the life of one of the women you studied. Have one group member narrate the skit as it is being performed.

4. In 1959 Ruth Handler designed the Barbie doll. Choose a famous American woman who you think should be honored with a doll. Explain your reasons on the back of a large paper-doll cutout that you decorate to look like her.

5. Susan Butcher bred, trained, and raced her dog teams to many Iditarod victories. Research this event and make a list of items that a sledder must pack for this almost 1,150-mile race.

6. Elizabeth Cochran, also known as Nellie Bly, asked to be locked up in prisons and insane asylums to learn how inmates were treated. Her resulting newspaper articles led to many reforms. Imagine a situation in which you have risked your life to help another person. Write a newspaper-style article describing this event.

7. Georgia O'Keeffe was an American painter famous for her still-life compositions presented in close-up views. Paint an O'Keeffe-style still life of any item in the classroom.

8. Cathy Guisewite is the creator of the cartoon strip "Cathy." Her cartoons make fun of the relationship Cathy has with her mother and boyfriend. Create and color a cartoon strip that shows a funny side to your relationship with a family member.

9. Rachel Carson's book *Silent Spring* raised awareness of the need to be good stewards of the earth. On a large circular cutout, write a paragraph that calls attention to an environmental problem that needs to be corrected. Color the remaining space on the circle so that it resembles Earth.

10. Barbara Walters is an American television journalist known for her ability to interview well-known figures and ask them point-blank questions. Choose a famous American woman whom you would like to interview; then list five questions that you would ask this person in the interview.

©The Education Center, Inc. • MARCH • TEC208

Note to the teacher: Fill in the due date on the contract before duplicating it. Give one copy of the contract to each student or group. Instruct students to color in the corresponding hat for each activity as it is completed.

Famous American Women

Business and Community Leaders
Antoinette Brown Blackwell • First official woman pastor in America (1852).
Mary Baker Eddy • Founder of Christian Science (1879).
Elizabeth Pinckney • Developer of indigo as a major commercial crop that helped our young country's economy.

Scientists and Inventors
Elizabeth Blackwell • First woman medical doctor in the United States (1849).
Annie Jump Cannon • Woman astronomer known for cataloging the stars.
Rachel Carson • Marine biologist who wrote *Silent Spring* and other books about ecology.
Dian Fossey • Zoologist who studied wild gorillas and found them to be gentle, social animals.
Alice Hamilton • Physician whose efforts to improve health conditions in industrial workplaces led to workers' compensation laws in the United States.
Grace Hopper • Mathematician who helped develop the language for the first commercial electronic computer.
Barbara McClintock • Geneticist who won the Nobel Prize in medicine (1983) for discovering earlier that genes transfer their positions on chromosomes.
Margaret Mead • Anthropologist known for her studies of primitive societies.
Maria Mitchell • Astronomer who was the first woman elected to the American Academy of Arts and Sciences (1848).
Florence Sabin • First woman elected to the National Academy of Sciences for her medical research.

Space Pioneers
Jacqueline Cochran • First woman to break the sound barrier (1953).
Amelia Earhart • First woman to fly across the Atlantic Ocean alone (1932).
Mae Jemison • First African-American woman in space (1992).
Christa McAuliffe • Selected to be the first "teacher in space" (1986).
Sally Ride • First American woman astronaut to participate in an orbital mission (1983).

Dancers
Agnes de Mille • Ballerina and choreographer for the New York City Ballet.
Ruth St. Denis • Cofounder of modern dance in America with Isadora Duncan.
Isadora Duncan • Creator of an expressive dance style and cofounder of modern dance in America with Ruth St. Denis.
Katherine Dunham • First black choreographer at the Metropolitan Opera in New York City (1963).
Martha Graham • Choreographer of American modern dance for more than 50 years.
Maria Tallchief • Greatly admired Native American ballerina who founded the Chicago City Ballet (1979).

Artists
Margaret Bourke-White • Major photographer and photojournalist.
Marcia Brown • Three-time winner of Caldecott Medal.
Mary Cassatt • Impressionist painter.
Barbara Cooney • Winner of Caldecott Medal (twice).
Cathy Guisewite • Cartoonist and creator of the cartoon strip "Cathy."
Malvina Hoffman • Sculptor best known for her 101 life-size bronzes, *Races of Man* (1932).
Georgia O'Keeffe • Abstract painter.

©The Education Center, Inc. • MARCH • TEC208

Note to the teacher: Use this list for additional studies. If desired, make a copy for each student. Also see the lists of other famous American women on pages 19–23.

Strengthening Measurement Skills

Do measurement skills weigh your students down? Then lighten their loads with the following exercises guaranteed to pump them up during National Weights and Measures Week (the first week in March) or any time of the year!

by Geri Harris, Judy Henline, and Marsha Schmus

Handy Hints and Useful Units
Creating nonstandard measurements

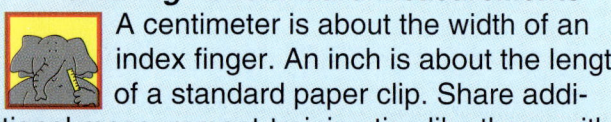
A centimeter is about the width of an index finger. An inch is about the length of a standard paper clip. Share additional measurement-training tips like these with students for times when rulers cannot be found. Next, challenge each child to find and list several objects that are approximately the same length as a foot, a yard, a meter, and a millimeter. Then have each student share his list of nonstandard units with other class members to make measurement easier for them, too! See the reproducible activity "How Do You Measure Up?" on page 36 for a great follow-up.

Walk a Mile in My Shoes
Identifying and using nonstandard measurements

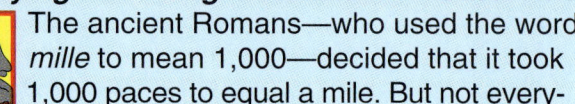
The ancient Romans—who used the word *mille* to mean 1,000—decided that it took 1,000 paces to equal a mile. But not everyone's *stride,* or long step, was the same length, so problems arose with this standard. Demonstrate this dilemma by having each student measure his stride.

First, use a 100-foot measuring tape to mark off a 66-foot length on the playground. Instruct each student to walk from one end of the length to the other end using a comfortable stride. Make sure he counts the number of strides it takes to walk one length. After repeating this process two times, have him find the average of his three walks. Finally, have him multiply that average by 80 to determine the number of strides it would take for him to walk a mile. Is the number close to 1,000?

Goofy Portraits
Using metric units of length

Listen for giggles as students complete this zany metric activity! Label eight containers as follows: Head Length, Head Width, Hair Length, Ear Length, Ear Width, Eye Width, Nose Length, and Mouth Width. Instruct each student to write these labels down the left side of a sheet of notebook paper. Fill each container with a class set of paper strips on which you have written a different metric length, such as 7 cm, 50 mm, 25 cm, or 1 dm. Have every student pull one strip from each container and write that dimension next to the appropriate label on her paper. Next, instruct the student to use colored paper, scissors, glue, markers, and metric rulers to construct a cut-paper portrait of an alien or monster. Stress that each student use the metric ruler to accurately measure her creature's features. Have each student label the creature's dimensions and then name and frame her goofy creation before displaying it on a bulletin board. If desired, have each student write a paragraph describing her metric monster.

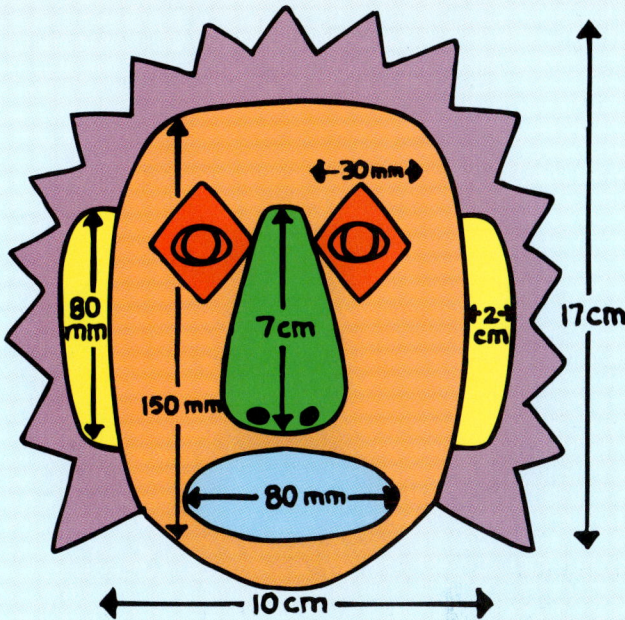

Suggested Widths and Lengths

2 dm	25 cm	10 mm	6 cm
18 cm	3 dm	1 dm	60 mm
150 mm	2.5 dm	90 mm	7 cm
15 cm	24 cm	2 cm	70 mm
200 mm	270 mm	20 mm	8 cm
16 cm	22 cm	3 cm	1.5 cm
1.5 dm	26 cm	30 mm	15 mm
110 mm	19 cm	4 cm	45 mm
120 mm	210 mm	5 cm	75 mm
13 cm	1 cm	50 mm	65 mm

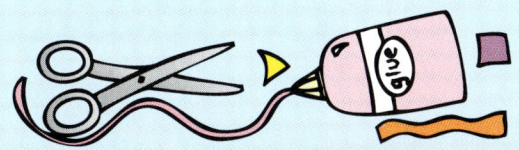

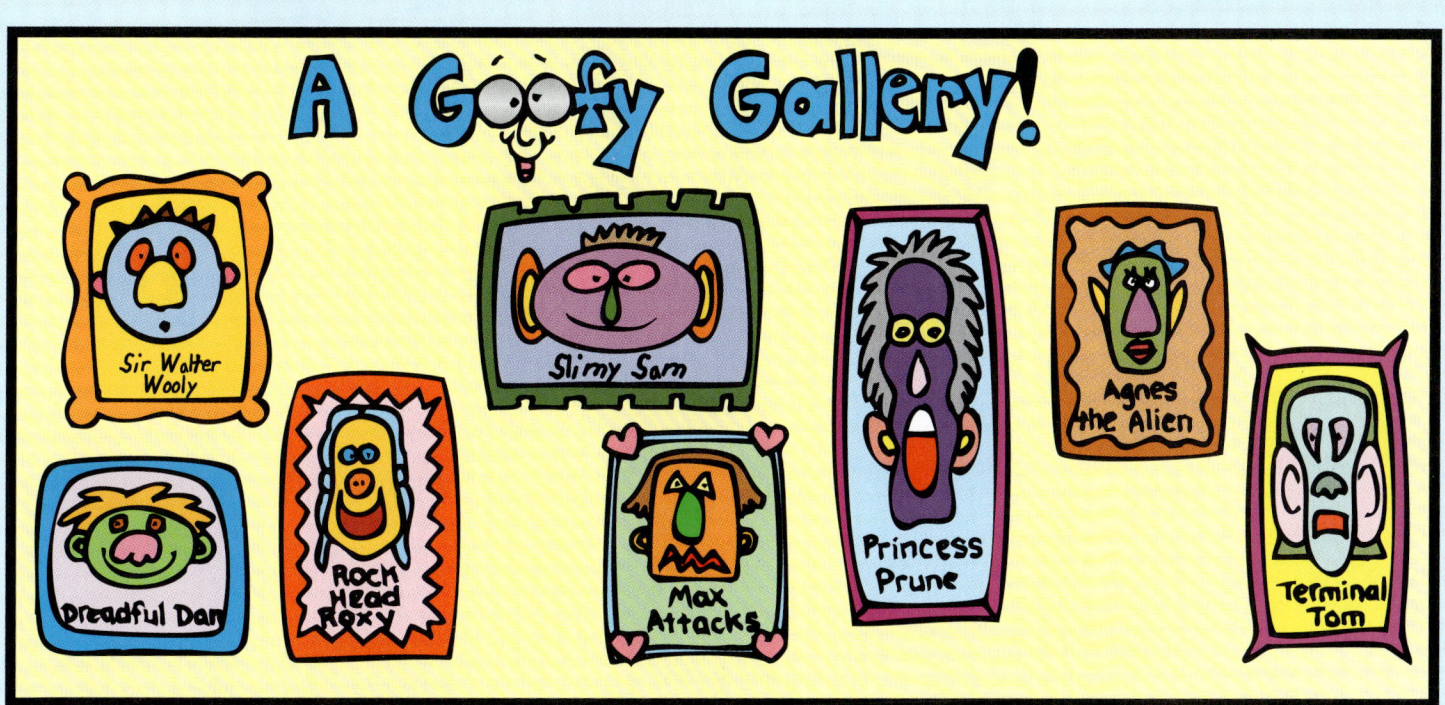

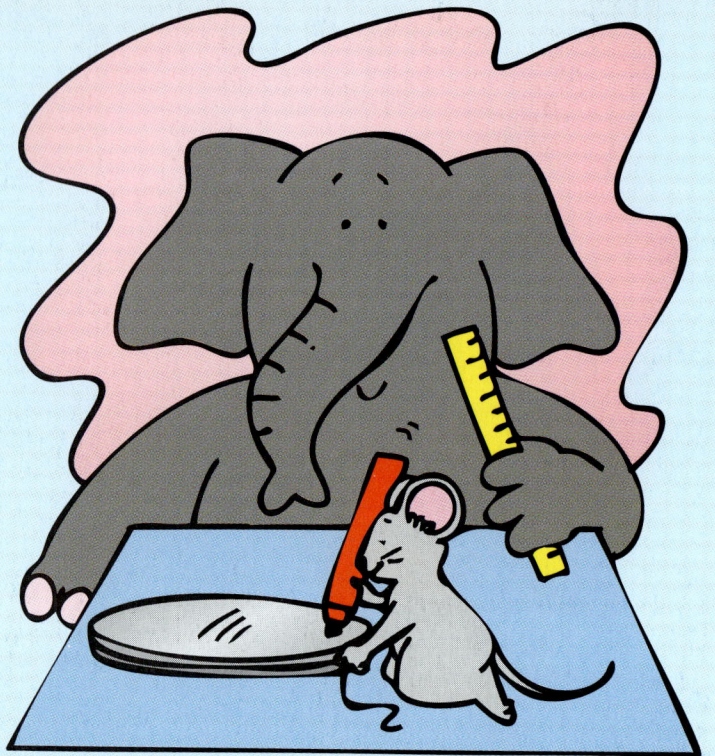

Measurement Scavenger Hunt
Using standard measurements

Strengthen your weight lifters' skills with a most unusual scavenger hunt. First, provide the following measuring tools in a central location in your class: rulers, yardsticks, a bathroom scale, a food scale (standard measurement), a two-cup measuring cup, and empty gallon jugs and quart containers. Next, duplicate the scavenger hunt form on page 38, one copy for each student in a pair. After discussing the directions on the sheet, encourage your hunting pairs to complete as many of the tasks on the form as possible within a 15-minute time period. Encourage students to find unusual objects to measure by informing them that teams win points only when the objects they measure differ from every other team's objects. When time expires, have student teams share their findings with the class; then award the points. The team with the most points wins.

Circles of Fun
Understanding circumference

Are you going around in circles trying to help students understand circumference? If so, try this simple hands-on activity. Have each student bring in the plastic lids from a variety of containers, such as coffee cans, potato-chip canisters, and margarine tubs. Pair students and give each pair a 24-inch length of string, a ruler, a lid, and a marker. Instruct the pair to wrap the string around the perimeter of the lid and mark the spot on the string where the two ends meet. Next, direct the pair to measure the distance between the two ends using a ruler. Provide additional practice by having the pairs exchange lids. Point out that the string method of finding circumference works well if the object is small. However, finding the circumference of a large object—such as a planet—requires the use of a special formula. Introduce students to the formula for finding circumference: diameter x π (π = 3.14). Have each pair figure the circumference of a lid using the string method and the formula. Compare the results to check for accuracy.

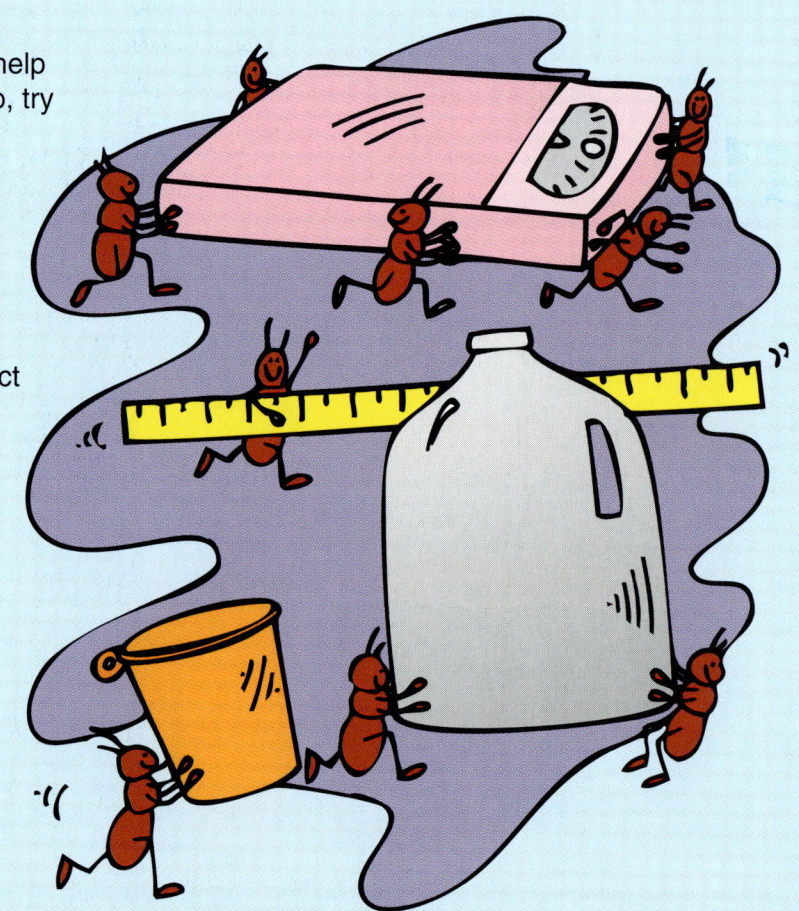

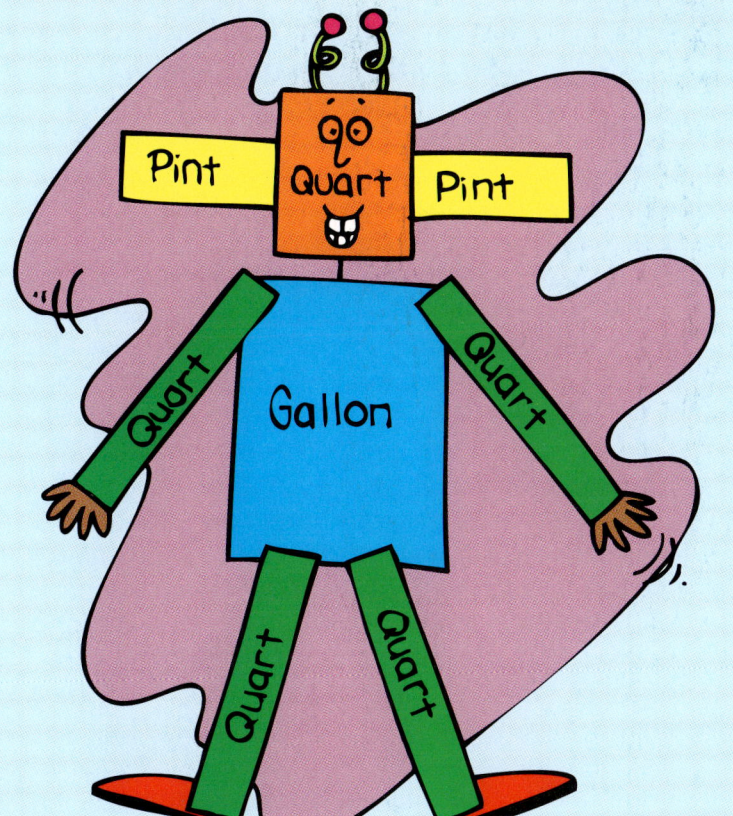

Measurement Bingo
Understanding standard and metric measurements

What better way to keep students' measurement skills fit than playing a fun game? Make a copy of the bingo gameboard on page 37 for each student. Also copy and cut apart the 24 measurement cards on the same page. Have each student write each of the following measurements in a separate box on his board (some of the measurements will be repeated): 1 ft., 1 yd., 1 mi., 2 ft., 2 yd., 1 cm, 1 dm, 1 m, 1 km, 2 dm, 2 m, 2 km, 5 dm, 5 m, 5 km, 1 yd., 1 mi., 2 yd., 1 dm, 1 m, 2 dm, 2 m, 5 dm, and 5 m. Distribute dried beans to students for covering the boxes during the game. To play, call out the measurement on one of the cards. Direct students to find the box containing an equivalent measurement on their gameboards and cover that box with a bean. The first student to cover five boxes in a row vertically, horizontally, or diagonally wins the round.

Measurement Models
Understanding standard measurements

Improve your students' measurement fitness with an exercise that becomes a fun visual activity. Have each student choose a category: length, capacity, or weight measurement. Then challenge each child to select two units from that category that have some proportional relationship to one another. For instance, two cups make one pint, or 12 inches make one foot, or 16 ounces make one pound. Next, have each student cut shapes from colorful paper that match the proportions of the units selected. Instruct the student to label each cutout as shown. After making a few sets of these relational cutouts, have the student combine them to construct a measurement character (see illustration). Display these colorful measurement models on a bulletin board to help the whole class review.

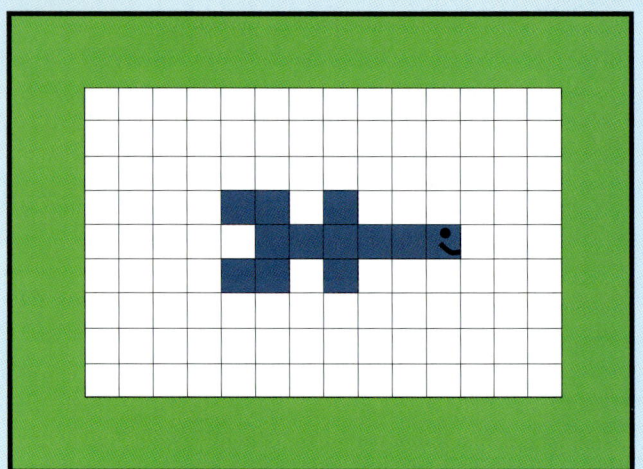

Crazy Creatures
Understanding and using area and perimeter

Delight students with a creative measurement activity that becomes a bulletin board. After studying area and perimeter, provide each student with a sheet of one-centimeter graph paper. Instruct the student to draw an animal with a body shape that has a perimeter of 26 units. Next, raise the difficulty level of the exercise by having each student create an animal with a designated perimeter *and* area. Instruct each student to label his creature and mount his graph on colorful paper. Display this collection of new life-forms on a bulletin board titled "Crazy Creatures."

Bowling for Meters
Adding metric units of length

Measurement vocabulary becomes as commonplace as bowling terms with this fun any-subject review. Label ten two-liter bottles with the following measurements: 1,000 mm, 1 m, 5 m, 100 cm, 50 dm, 300 cm, 10 dm, 2 m, 200 cm, and 20 dm. Arrange the bottles like bowling pins at one end of the room. Use tape to mark a bowling line that is three meters from the bottles. Divide the class into two teams; then have each team select a representative. Ask team A a question and allow time for members to confer. Then have team A's representative give the team's answer. If the spokesperson responds correctly, direct one of team A's members to stand behind the bowling line and roll a softball toward the bottles. Instruct team A to total and record the measurements written on the toppled bottles. Continue the game by directing the next question to team B and so on. Remind each team to keep a running score, and check each team's totals for correctness. If a team's representative answers a question incorrectly, allow the opposing team to give the answer and bowl. Alternate turns after each correct answer. The first team to score a total of 50 meters wins.

How High Is It?
Determining heights of tall objects, using a theodolite

Surveyors use a special instrument called a *theodolite* to measure heights accurately. Help students understand how the heights of tall objects like mountains are measured. Duplicate the directions below and page 39 for each pair of students. After each student has constructed a theodolite, take the children outside and have each child practice using the instrument with his partner. As a class, measure a common object such as a flagpole. Check student responses for accuracy; then have each pair use page 39 and the theodolites to measure and record the heights of trees and other tall objects.

How to Construct a *Theodolite*

Have you ever wondered how the height of a mountain is measured? A surveyor uses a special instrument called a *theodolite* to measure the height of a tall object accurately. Use the following directions to help each of you make a simple version of this tool.

Materials for two theodolites:
6" square of stiff cardboard, cut in half diagonally
2 plastic straws
two 10" lengths of thread
2 metal screws
transparent tape

Directions for making a theodolite:
1. Tape one straw onto the longest side of one of the cardboard triangles.
2. Tie one of the screws to the end of the thread as shown.
3. Tape the other end of the thread to the cardboard under the top end of the straw so that the thread hangs straight down along the edge of the triangle as shown.

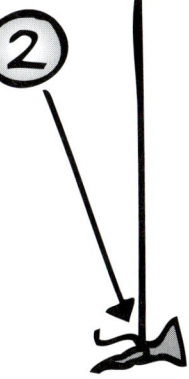

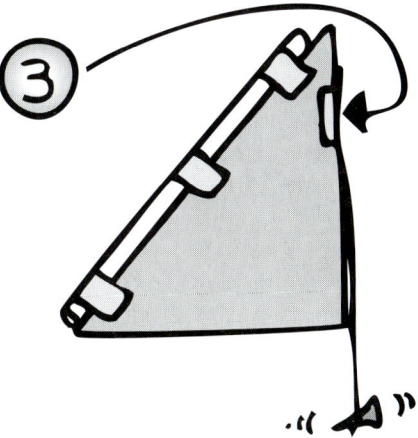

Name _____   Nonstandard measurement

How Do You Measure Up?

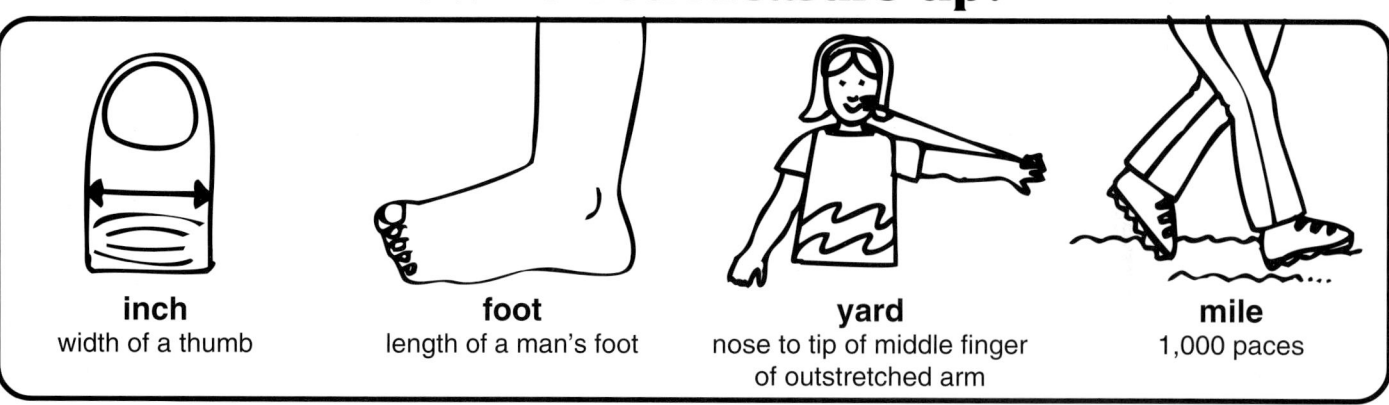

inch
width of a thumb

foot
length of a man's foot

yard
nose to tip of middle finger of outstretched arm

mile
1,000 paces

In earlier times people used different parts of their bodies to measure length. Do the activities in Parts A and B below to help your measurement skills grow.

Part A: Work with four of your classmates. Use a tape measure to measure the width of the thumb and the lengths of or distances between the other body parts listed below. To measure a *stride* (long step), place the tape measure at the back of the heel of one foot. Then measure to the heel of the other foot. Record your measurements in the chart below.

What to Measure	Student 1	Student 2	Student 3	Student 4	Student 5
Thumb					
Foot					
Nose to Fingertip of Outstretched Arm					
Stride From Heel to Heel					

What observations can you make about the accuracy of your measurements? _____

_____

_____

Part B: Invent your own measuring device. Without using standard measuring tools, find the heights of yourself and your classmates from Part A above.

	Student 1	Student 2	Student 3	Student 4	Student 5
Height in _____ (nonstandard unit)					

Bonus Box: Each of the following terms relates to some form of measurement. Use a dictionary to tell what each one measures: knot, fathom, watt, speedometer, odometer.

©The Education Center, Inc. • MARCH • TEC208 • Key p. 92

Note to the teacher: Use this reproducible to follow up "Handy Hints and Useful Units" on page 30. Make one copy for each student.

24 inches	2,000 meters	36 inches
3 feet	12 inches	5,280 feet
1,760 yards	10 centimeters	100 millimeters
20 decimeters	200 centimeters	50 decimeters
500 centimeters	10 decimeters	100 centimeters
200 millimeters	20 centimeters	6 feet
72 inches	10 millimeters	5,000 meters
50 centimeters	500 millimeters	1,000 meters

B I N G O

		FREE SPACE		

Note to the teacher: Use the bingo gameboard and measurement cards with "Measurement Bingo" on page 33. Duplicate the gameboard for each student. Make one copy of the cards—laminating them if desired before cutting them apart.

Measurement Scavenger Hunt

You are about to embark on a very interesting search. Read through the list below. Then search the classroom for one unusual object to match each given measurement.

Find an item that…

Remember: You earn a point for each object only if your answer is correct *and* is not mentioned by someone else!

1. is less than 8 inches long: _____
2. is more than 1 foot long: _____
3. is less than 3/4 inch long: _____
4. is about 1 yard long: _____
5. weighs more than 1 pound: _____
6. weighs about an ounce: _____
7. weighs about the same amount as you: _____
8. holds about 1 gallon of liquid: _____
9. holds about 1 quart of liquid: _____
10. holds about 1 pint of liquid: _____

Name(s) _____   Measuring a tall object

A Tall Task

Here's an activity that will really keep you looking up! Work with your partner to measure a tall tree or other tall object. Follow the directions below and use your theodolites. Record your findings on this page.

How to measure with the theodolite:
1. Have your partner measure your height.
2. Pick out the object you want to measure.
3. Look through the straw at your object while holding the theodolite so that the thread hangs straight down along the edge of the cardboard triangle. Ask for your partner's help with this.
4. Still looking through the straw, move forward or backward until you see the top of your object. Have your partner mark the spot where you finally stand.
5. Measure the distance from where you stand to the bottom of the object. Add this distance to your height to determine the height of the object. For example, if a tree is 30 feet away and you are five feet tall, the height of the tree is 35 feet.
6. Help your partner measure the height of the same object. If you and your partner have the same answer, then you probably have measured correctly.

Data
1. Height of student A _____ : _____
   (Name of Student)

2. Distance from student A to the object: _____

3. Height of student A plus the distance to the object (#1 + #2): _____

4. Height of the object: _____

5. Height of student B _____ : _____
   (Name of Student)

6. Distance from student B to the object: _____

7. Height of student B plus the distance to the object (#5 + #6): _____

8. Height of the object: _____

Bonus Box: Measure the height of another tall object, such as a flagpole, telephone pole, or building.

©The Education Center, Inc. • *MARCH* • TEC208

Note to the teacher: Use this reproducible with "How High Is It?" on page 35. Each student will need a pencil, a yardstick or measuring tape, and the theodolite that she constructed.

Name _____   Measurement, problem solving

Deep-Sea Measuring

Do you enjoy riddles? Study the information in the chart. Then read each of the clues below. Use the data in the chart to help you identify the deep-sea dwellers described below.

Dolphin	Length	Shark	Length	Whale	Length
Bottle-nosed Dolphin	12 ft.	Bull Shark	11 ft.	Blue Whale	98 ft.
Spinner Dolphin	7 ft.	Scalloped Hammerhead Shark	13 ft. 9 in.	Humpback Whale	53 ft.
Striped Dolphin	9 ft.	Tiger Shark	18 ft.	Killer Whale	31 ft.
		White Shark	21 ft.		

1. I am 12 inches shorter than the bottle-nosed dolphin. Who am I? _____
2. I am 540 inches shorter than the blue whale. Who am I? _____
3. I am 4 yards 1 foot longer than the tiger shark. Who am I? _____
4. I am 2 yards longer than the bottle-nosed dolphin. Who am I? _____
5. I am 165 inches long. Who am I? _____
6. I am 48 inches shorter than the bull shark. Who am I? _____
7. I am 1 yard longer than the striped dolphin. Who am I? _____
8. I am 24 inches longer than the spinner dolphin. Who am I? _____
9. I am 1,176 inches long. Who am I? _____
10. I am 7 feet 3 inches longer than the scalloped hammerhead shark. Who am I? _____
11. I am half as long as a tiger shark. Who am I? _____
12. I am about eight times longer than the bottle-nosed dolphin. Who am I? _____
13. We are the closest in length. Who are we?   _____ and _____
14. Our combined lengths equal the length of a tiger shark. Who are we?

    _____ and _____

15. It would take about nine of me to equal the length of a blue whale. Who am I? _____

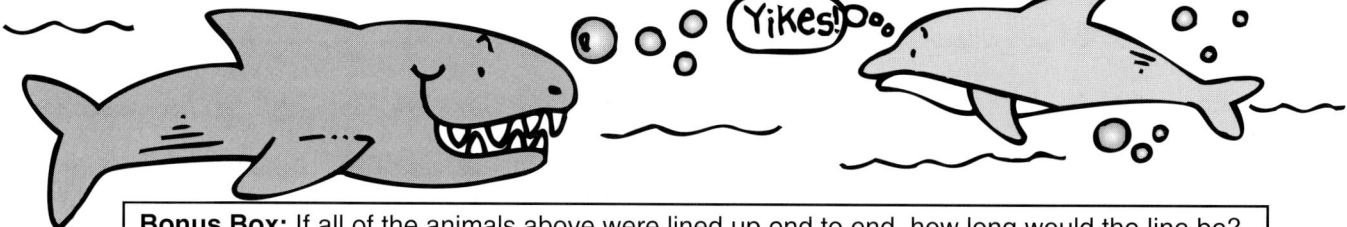

Bonus Box: If all of the animals above were lined up end to end, how long would the line be?

Name _____   *Measuring elapsed time*

Freddie's Fun Center

Plan to spend a fun-filled day at Freddie's Fun Center. Look at the list of activities you can enjoy. Notice that the chart gives the number of tickets needed for each activity and the time required to complete each one. You have four hours to do as much as you can. But remember these important things as you plan your exciting day:

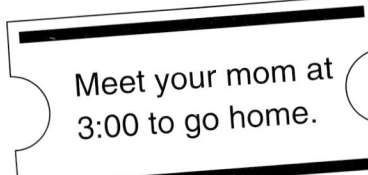
Meet your mom at 3:00 to go home.

Begin your first activity at 11:00.

Use *all* 24 of your tickets.

Stay as busy as possible. (You can rest later!)

Take some time to eat the lunch you brought.

Activity	Time Required	Tickets Needed Per Person
Miniature Golf	45 minutes	4
Baseball Pitch	15 minutes	2
Go-Carts	20 minutes	3
Arcade Games	25 minutes	3
Water Slide	40 minutes	4
Skee Ball	30 minutes	2
Pony Ride	10 minutes	2

Fill in the chart below to plan your day:

Time	Activity	Time Needed	Tickets Needed
11:00 A.M.			
3:00 P.M.			

Bonus Box: Use the back of this sheet to plan another fun-filled day. Plan to stay for only two hours. What is the greatest number of activities you can fit into two hours without repeating any activity? How many tickets will you need?

©The Education Center, Inc. • *MARCH* • TEC208 • Key p. 92   41

Name(s) _____ Measurement game

Test Your Memory!

Test the strength of your memory! Pair up with a partner to help you learn the units of measurement. Follow the directions below to become a master of measurement!

Directions:
1. Cut out the playing cards below. Then shuffle them and spread them out face-down on your desk.
2. Have Player A turn over two cards. Look at the Table of Measures at right to see if the cards match (equal the same measurement). If the cards make a match, Player A keeps both cards and takes another turn. If the cards do not match, Player A turns the cards back over and Player B takes a turn.
3. The game ends when all the cards have been chosen. The player with the most cards wins.

Table of Measures
2 cups = 1 pint
2 pints = 1 quart
4 cups = 1 quart or 2 pints
4 quarts = 1 gallon
1 foot = 12 inches
1 yard = 36 inches or 3 feet
1 mile = 1,760 yards or 5,280 feet
16 ounces = 1 pound
2,000 pounds = 1 ton

4 cups	1 quart	2 cups	1 pint	2 pints	1 quart
4 quarts	1 gallon	16 ounces	1 pound	2,000 pounds	1 ton
1 mile	5,280 feet	1 yard	36 inches	1 foot	12 inches
1 mile	1,760 yards	1 quart	2 pints	3 feet	1 yard

©The Education Center, Inc. • MARCH • TEC208

Note to the teacher: Duplicate this page for each pair of students. Provide each pair with scissors.

Name ______________________ *Exact measurement, fractions*

Cracking the Ruler Code

Bruno and his friend want to meet at the roller rink for some exercise. To keep Bruno's pesky little brother from finding out, they made the plans using a "Ruler Code." Study the rulers below and decode the boys' messages.

1. I will meet you at ___ ___ ___ ___ ___ ___ ___ ___ ___ ___ ___.
$1\frac{1}{2}$ $2\frac{3}{4}$ 1 $\frac{3}{8}$ $3\frac{1}{2}$ $4\frac{7}{8}$ 6 $1\frac{3}{4}$ 4 $4\frac{7}{8}$ $\frac{1}{8}$

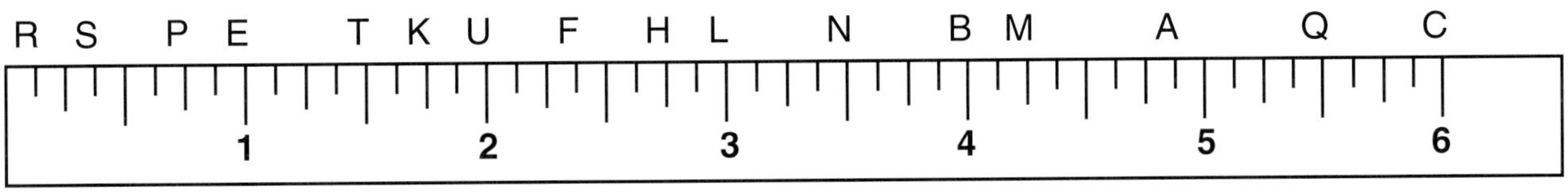

2. Don't forget to bring your ___ ___ ___ ___ ___ ___ ___ ___ ___.
$1\frac{3}{8}$ $3\frac{3}{8}$ $2\frac{5}{8}$ 5 6 $5\frac{3}{4}$ $1\frac{7}{8}$ $3\frac{1}{4}$ $2\frac{3}{4}$

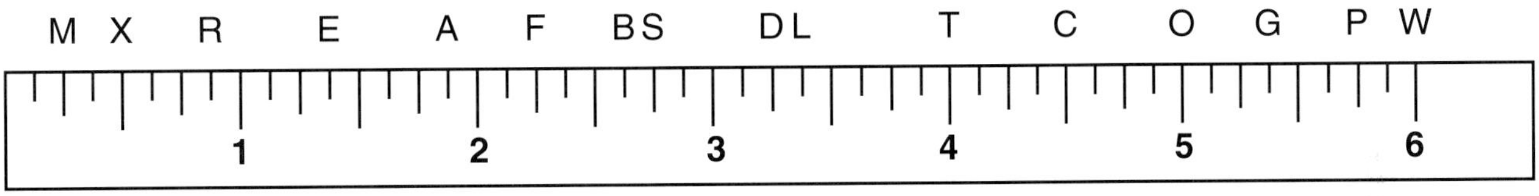

3. Bring some money to ___ ___ ___ ___ ___ ___ ___ ___ ___ ___ ___ ___.
$3\frac{1}{2}$ $2\frac{1}{4}$ $\frac{4}{8}$ $5\frac{1}{4}$ 4 $2\frac{3}{4}$ $2\frac{1}{4}$ 1 $5\frac{1}{2}$ $1\frac{2}{8}$ $1\frac{2}{8}$ $1\frac{3}{4}$

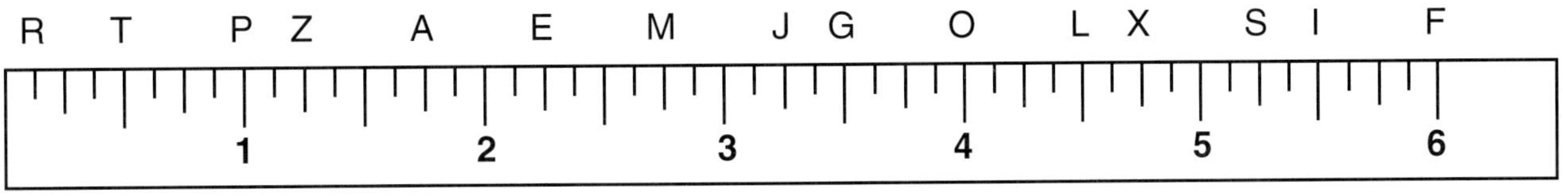

4. I might bring ___ ___ ___ ___ ___ ___ ___ ___ ___ ___ ___ ___ ___.
$1\frac{1}{2}$ $\frac{3}{4}$ 5 $2\frac{1}{4}$ $3\frac{3}{8}$ 4 $4\frac{1}{2}$ $\frac{2}{8}$ $2\frac{1}{2}$ 6 $3\frac{1}{8}$ $3\frac{1}{8}$ $\frac{3}{4}$

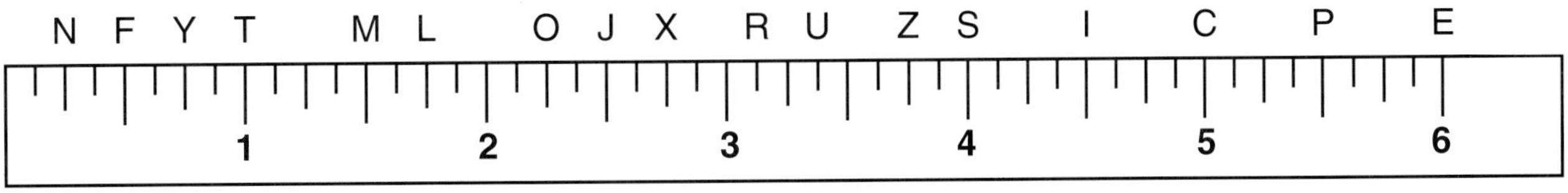

5. I need to be home ___ ___ ___ ___ ___ ___.
4 $1\frac{1}{8}$ $1\frac{1}{4}$ $2\frac{5}{8}$ $2\frac{1}{4}$ $5\frac{1}{2}$

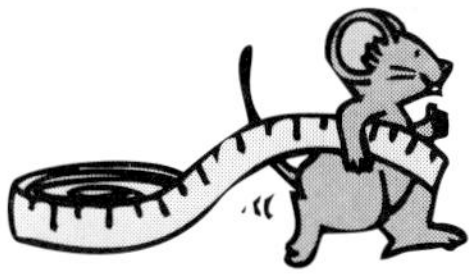

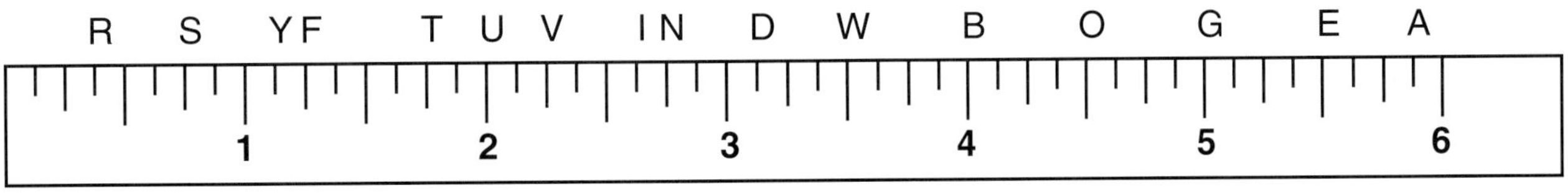

Bonus Box: Choose one of the rulers above and use its letters to write a ruler-code message to a friend. Then give the message to the friend to solve.

Leapin' Leprechauns!

Capture the luck of the Irish during the month of March! Use these activities to get your "little leprechauns" thinking critically and creatively about St. Patrick's Day!

by Elizabeth H. Lindsay and Debra Liverman

The Origins of St. Patrick's Day
Building background information

Long ago, the Irish set aside March 17 to honor St. Patrick, the priest who brought Christianity to Ireland. The day commemorates his death in the year 461. It became a custom to wear a sprig of shamrock on this day because legend states that St. Patrick used this *trifolium* (clover) to explain the meaning of the Holy Trinity to the people. In time, the holiday was not only a religious celebration, but also a festival of spring and of Ireland's independence from British rule.

The Wearin' of the Green
Critical thinking, writing for a purpose

Put on those green thinking caps for this thought-provoking activity! Have students brainstorm a list of the various holidays we celebrate and the colors associated with them. Talk about why we associate a particular color with a specific holiday. For example, we associate green with St. Patrick's Day because it is symbolic of the color of Ireland.

Next, have students imagine what it would be like if a law were passed in their town making it illegal to wear or display green on St. Patrick's Day. Discuss the problems that would arise from such a law. Ask students: "How would the general public react? How do you think it might make Irish-Americans feel? How would this affect local businesses?" Direct each student to respond to these questions by writing a letter to the editor of an imaginary newspaper, *The Shamrock Times*. In his letter, have him respond from the point of view of an Irish-American, a local businessman, or a student from Great Britain.

The Spirit of St. Patrick
Understanding the significance of a holiday, writing for a purpose

St. Patrick is honored by the Irish because of the many brave and kind deeds he performed for the people. He traveled the countryside sharing his beliefs about God, and he built churches and schools. Because he spent his life caring for the people of Ireland, the Irish celebrate and honor him on March 17. Get your students into the true spirit of St. Patrick's Day by having them perform their own special deeds. Have each student choose a person in the classroom or school to whom he would like to offer an act of kindness. Suggest the following: help a classmate who is experiencing difficulty in a subject, clean classroom for a busy teacher, or read to a student in a lower grade. Make a copy of the shamrock pattern on page 49 for each student. Have him write to the person describing the act of kindness he will perform. Have the student finish the shamrock by decorating and delivering it. Both sender and receiver will feel good about the kindhearted deed.

A Rainbow of Reviews
Motivating students to read, responding to literature

Is there no pot of gold at the end of the rainbow when it comes to getting your students into reading? Use this motivating bulletin board idea for help. Draw a large pot on one side of the bulletin board paper. Paint a colorful rainbow directly onto the background paper. Use the coin pattern on page 48 to add some gold to your pot. The rest is up to your students! Have each child set a reading goal for the month. After a book is read, instruct the student to write a review on a coin pattern plucked from the pot on your bulletin board. Staple each review along the rainbow. As soon as her reading goal is met, have the student flip a coin to choose a treat—heads earns free time and tails a piece of candy!

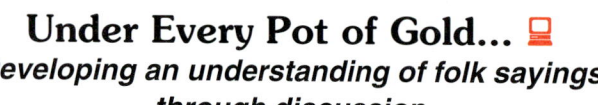

Under Every Pot of Gold...
Developing an understanding of folk sayings through discussion

The Irish are full of wit and wisdom! The following are some well-known Irish sayings. Put students in cooperative groups to discuss the literal meaning of each saying and when each would be used. Then have each group determine the deeper meaning of each saying. Discuss each group's interpretations; then have each student write about a time when one of these sayings fit a situation in his life. Add a "touch o' humor" by having the student write his anecdote on an illustration of the saying.

- A shut mouth catches no flies.
- In the world of the blind the one-eyed man is king.
- A full cabin is better than an empty castle.
- You can't find a thing except in the place it is.
- Often a person's mouth has broken his nose.
- He who has water and peat on his farm has the world.
- The people go, but the hills remain.
- Don't desert the highway for the shortcut.
- A blessing does not fill the belly.

The Luck of the Irish!
Developing an understanding of folklore through discussion, writing for a purpose

When was the last time you heard someone say, "Boy, are you lucky!" Lucky charms, hats, socks, and coins are kept by people everywhere. In Irish lore, if you catch a leprechaun, he is supposed to lead you to a pot of gold. The four-leaf clover is supposed to bring good luck to its finder. Discuss with your students questions such as these: What is luck? Is there really such a thing? Why doesn't it work all of the time? Ask students what items they have that they consider lucky, and why they feel these items bring them luck. Give each student a copy of the shamrock pattern on page 49. On her pattern, have each student write the name of an item that she considers lucky. Then instruct her to describe what makes the item a lucky object. Or vary the assignment by having each student describe why she thinks she is a lucky person. Display the completed patterns on a wall or bulletin board titled "Shamrocks and Shillelaghs."

Food for Thought
Experiencing a cultural tradition

Potatoes have long been an important ingredient in Irish recipes because they are tasty and easy to grow, harvest, and cook. Prepare the following traditional Irish foods for your class to enjoy. Serve the dishes with the customary glass of milk. Give each student a copy of each recipe so he can see what actually went into the festive treats. Use the recipes as an opportunity for practicing following directions and reviewing fractions. Have each student halve or double the recipes and rewrite the ingredients.

Potato Soup
3 oz. butter
2 lb. potatoes, peeled and diced
2 large onions, diced
5 c. water
3 tbsp. mixed dried herbs (i.e., parsley, thyme, and sage)
salt and pepper to taste
1 1/4 c. milk
2 tbsp. cream
2 tbsp. chopped chives or green onions

Melt the butter in a pan and slowly simmer the potatoes and onions. Do not brown. Add the water, herbs, salt, and pepper, and continue to simmer on low heat until the vegetables are tender (about 1/2 hour). Stir in the milk. Heat thoroughly. Remove from the heat and allow to cool. To make creamy and smooth, put the mixture through a blender before adding the cream and chives (or green onions). If you do not blend the soup, serve hot, garnishing with cream and chives.

Potato Cakes
1/4 c. butter
3/4 c. white flour
1/2 tsp. salt
1/2 tsp. baking powder
3 c. freshly mashed potatoes (with milk)

Cut butter into flour until it forms large granules. Add salt and baking powder; mix well. Mix in potatoes. Knead for a few minutes. Roll out onto lightly floured board with floured rolling pin. Cut into four rounds. Cook on a lightly buttered griddle or skillet until brown on both sides. Serve hot.

Graph It!
Collecting and graphing data

Holidays provide a great opportunity to practice those graphing skills, and St. Patrick's Day is no exception! Some possibilities include the following:

- Have each student choose five people to watch for two days. Instruct the student to see how many wear green on March 17; then see how many wear green on March 18. Have the student graph the findings of the two sets of data. Circle graphs and double bar graphs work well.
- Divide the class into five cooperative groups. Assign each group one of the following fun questions:
  — What is the first thing you think of when you visualize the color green?
  — What is your favorite holiday?
  — From which country(ies) do your ancestors come?
  — What is your favorite green vegetable?
  — How do you like your potatoes cooked?

  Instruct each group to survey its classmates. On a large sheet of chart paper, have each group graph its results. Share the results by hanging the charts on a wall titled "Fun Fact Findings."
- Have your students give another class a "St. Patrick's Day Quick Quiz" to see how much they know about this holiday. Help students create five to ten multiple-choice quiz questions, such as "Where was St. Patrick born? (a) Ireland, (b) Africa, or (c) Britain." Enlist a student to type and a couple of others to edit the quiz. Make multiple copies and have a small group of students travel to the different classes to distribute the quizzes. After checking the answers, have students tally the results of each question, then graph the results using percentages.

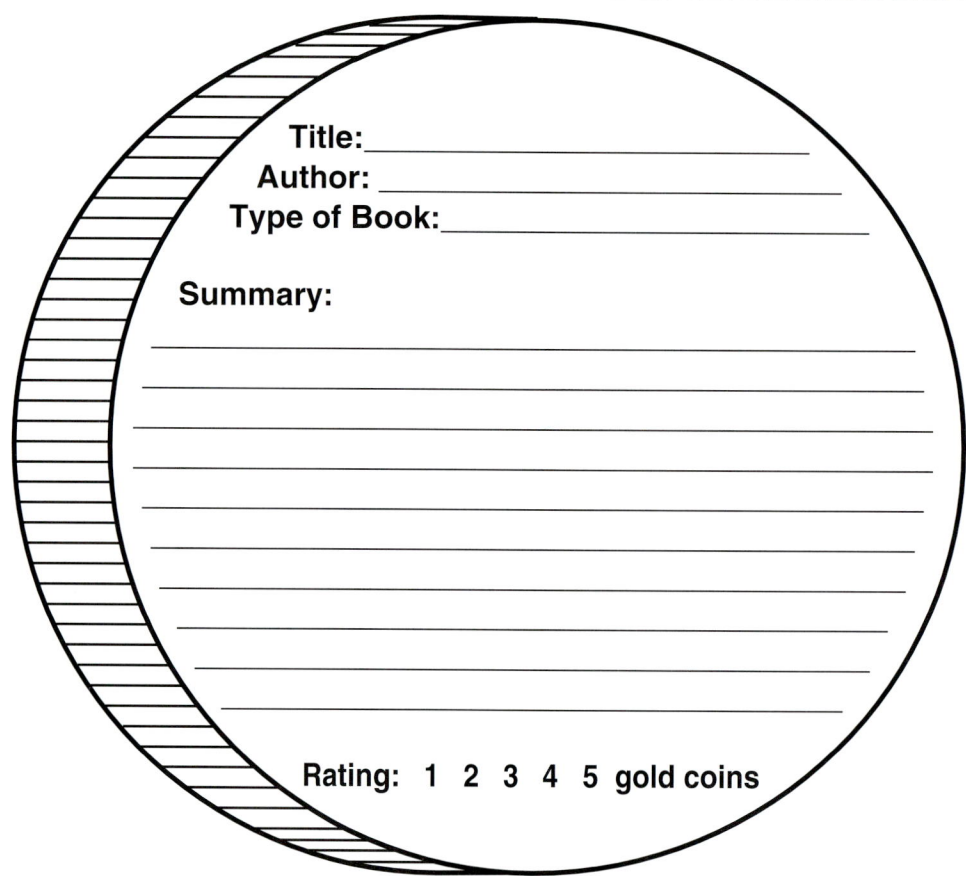

©The Education Center, Inc. • MARCH • TEC208

Note to the teacher: Make multiple copies of the pattern for each student to use with "A Rainbow of Reviews" on page 45.

Pattern
Use with "The Spirit of St. Patrick" on page 45 and "The Luck of the Irish!" on page 46.

Name _____

St. Patrick's Day: contract

Golden Opportunities

The Irish say that if you catch a leprechaun and keep your eye on him, he must lead you to a pot of gold! Read all of the following activities. Choose _____ coins to complete. See how much gold you can collect with your knowledge of St. Patrick's Day!

Due date: _____

 **1.** St. Patrick is the reason for this March holiday. Research ten facts about his early life. Draw a picture illustrating the facts. Create a jigsaw puzzle by cutting the picture into interlocking pieces. Share your puzzle with a friend.

 **2.** One legend about St. Patrick says that he drove all the snakes out of Ireland. Choose a breed of snake found in the United States to research. Include such information as the size, characteristics, habitat, and diet of the snake. Report your findings on a life-sized drawing of the snake.

 **4.** Ireland was the first country in Europe to grow potatoes as a major crop. Prepare your favorite dish made with potatoes, and bring it in for the whole class to enjoy. Be sure to bring in a copy of the recipe to share with your classmates.

 **5.** Read about the life of St. Patrick. Draw and cut out each of the letters that spell his name. On each letter write an adjective that describes him. Add a sentence telling why you chose that adjective. Connect the letters by hole-punching the tops and stringing them together with a piece of yarn.

 **6.** One legend about St. Patrick states that the sun didn't set for 12 days and nights after his death. Pretend you are a reporter and write a newspaper article reporting the details of this astounding event.

 **7.** The Irish flag is divided into three equal vertical sections of orange, white, and green. Divide a piece of white paper into three equal parts. Research the meaning behind each of these colors and record it in the appropriate section; then color each section of the flag.

 **8.** Although St. Patrick was not born in Ireland, it became his adopted country. Draw and label a map of the Emerald Isle. Include information about its size in square miles, population, major cities, bodies of water, and resources. Add a compass rose and a key to your map.

Note to the teacher: Program a copy of this contract with the required number of activities and the due date. Make one copy for each student.

Name _____ *Analogies*

Parading Through Analogies

By the end of the 1850s, a St. Patrick's Day parade was held every year in cities across the United States. So hop on the float and parade on through this page of analogies! Read each sentence. Figure out the relationship of the boldface pair of words and then apply it to find the analogy of the italicized word. May the luck of the Irish be with you!

sample: **Pixie** is to **imaginary** as *mouse* is to _____real_____.

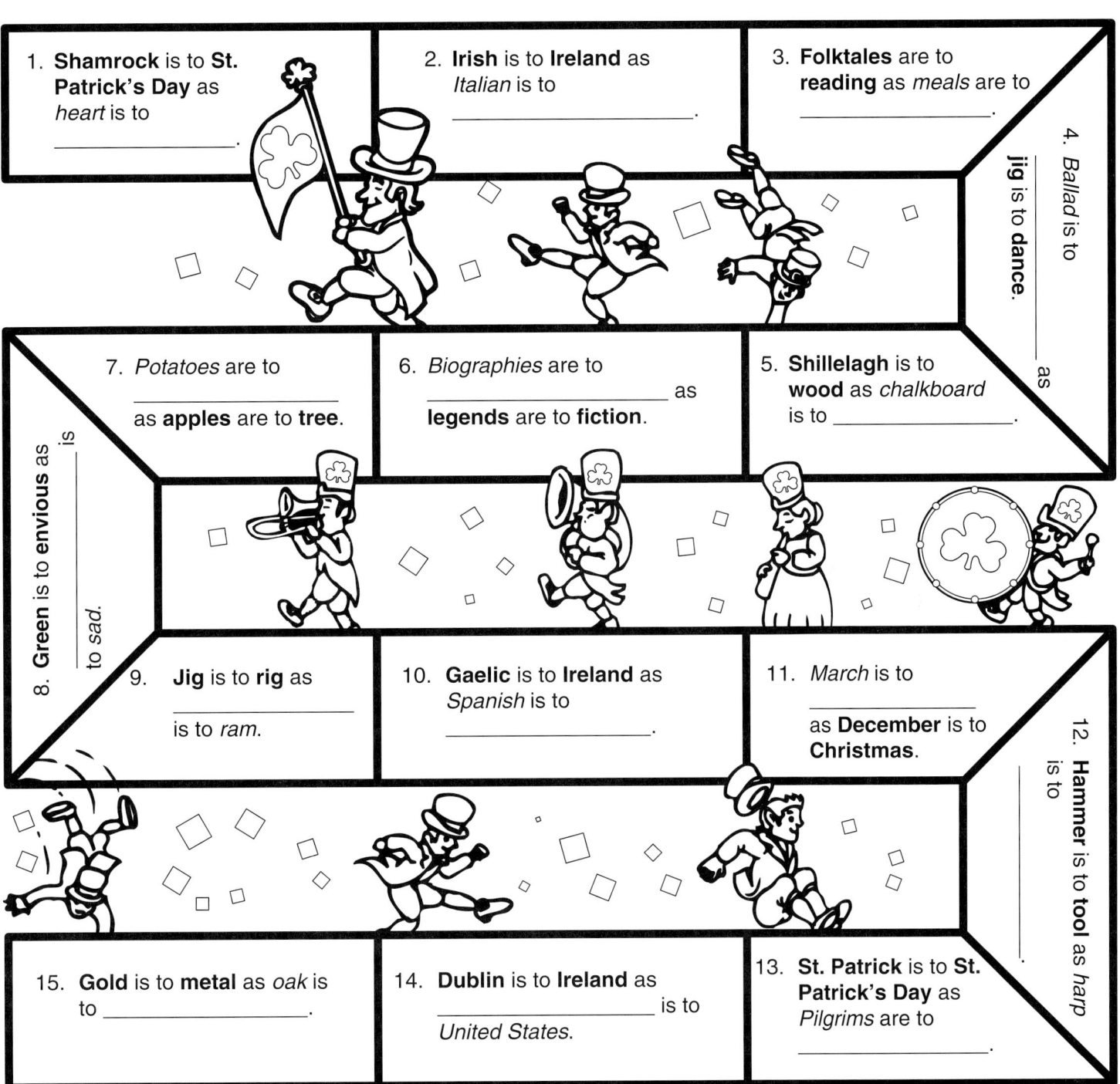

1. **Shamrock** is to **St. Patrick's Day** as *heart* is to _____.

2. **Irish** is to **Ireland** as *Italian* is to _____.

3. **Folktales** are to **reading** as *meals* are to _____.

4. *Ballad* is to _____ as **jig** is to **dance**.

5. **Shillelagh** is to **wood** as *chalkboard* is to _____.

6. *Biographies* are to _____ as **legends** are to **fiction**.

7. *Potatoes* are to _____ as **apples** are to **tree**.

8. **Green** is to **envious** as _____ is to *sad*.

9. **Jig** is to **rig** as _____ is to *ram*.

10. **Gaelic** is to **Ireland** as *Spanish* is to _____.

11. *March* is to _____ as **December** is to **Christmas**.

12. **Hammer** is to **tool** as *harp* is to _____.

13. **St. Patrick** is to **St. Patrick's Day** as *Pilgrims* are to _____.

14. **Dublin** is to **Ireland** as _____ is to *United States*.

15. **Gold** is to **metal** as *oak* is to _____.

Bonus Box: Each statement above contains a word related to St. Patrick's Day. Write a silly story on the back of this page using all of the related words.

Leprechaun Logic

The local leprechaun family plans a traditional Irish party each year for St. Patrick's Day. Six leprechauns were given jobs to do to help prepare for this year's event. Larry has lost the list that tells them who is supposed to do each job! To help them figure out who is responsible for each task, put an O on the grid to match each leprechaun to the correct job. (Hint: To help solve the puzzle, make an X to indicate the jobs that are not the leprechaun's responsibility.)

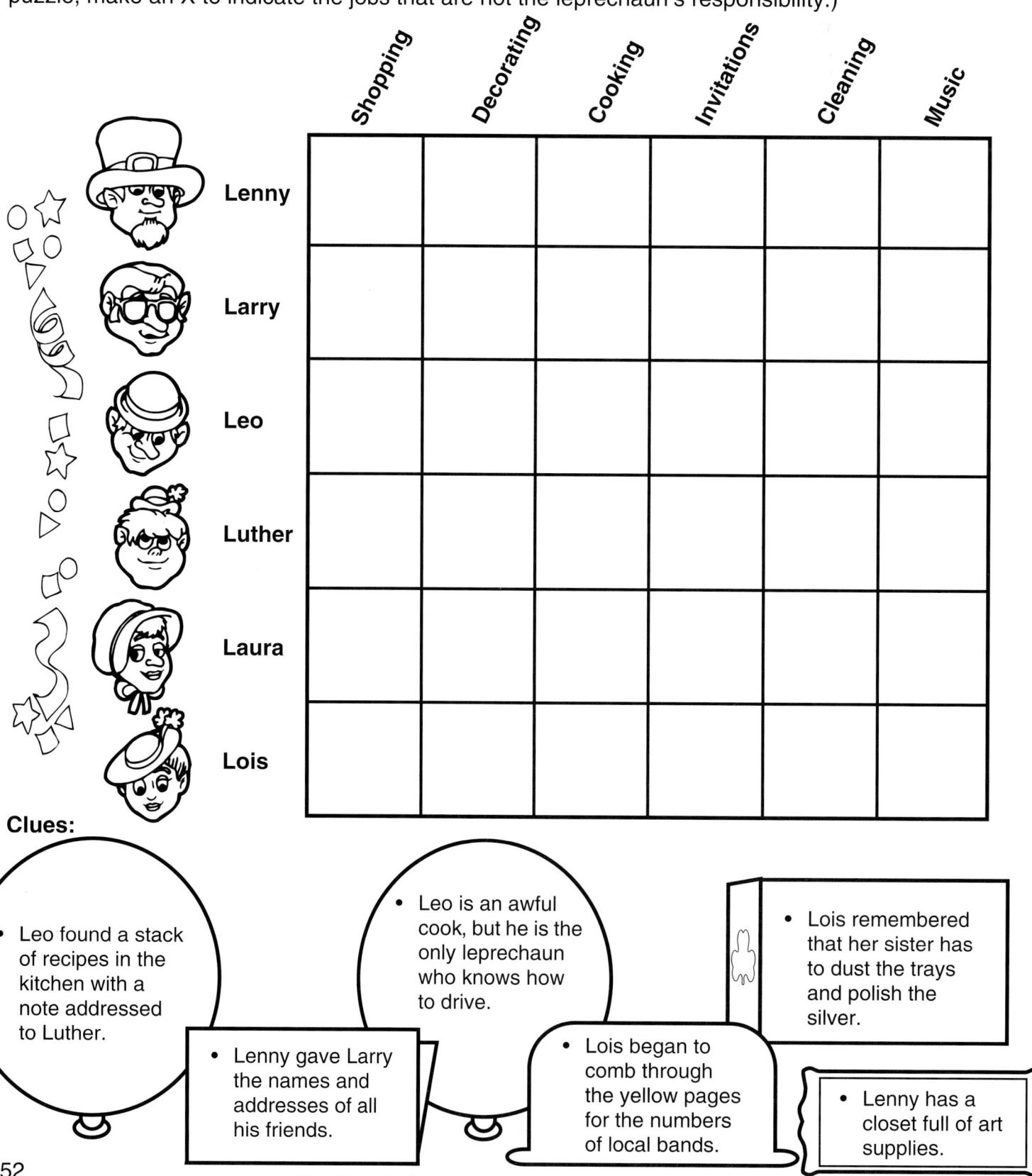

Clues:

- Leo found a stack of recipes in the kitchen with a note addressed to Luther.

- Leo is an awful cook, but he is the only leprechaun who knows how to drive.

- Lenny gave Larry the names and addresses of all his friends.

- Lois began to comb through the yellow pages for the numbers of local bands.

- Lois remembered that her sister has to dust the trays and polish the silver.

- Lenny has a closet full of art supplies.

Name _____   Problem solving

"Tri" This

You've probably used Venn diagrams before, but have you ever used them in math? The use of diagrams is a great way to solve problems. Use what you know about these joining circles to help figure out the problems below. Be sure to fill each region of the circles with the correct number.

1. Students from Ms. Hubal's class were surveyed to see who believes in leprechauns, Santa Claus, or both. Of the 30 students polled, 12 believe in Santa Claus, 24 believe in leprechauns, and 6 believe in both.

   How many students believe in Santa Claus only? How many students believe in leprechauns only?

2. Leslie O'Connor, a fifth-grade student, polled 77 fourth graders to find out what each knew about the life of St. Patrick. Forty-three students knew where he was born; 51 knew what he was famous for; 42 knew what his job was; 15 knew where he was born and what he was famous for; 10 knew where he was born and what his job was; 12 knew what he was famous for and what his job was; 11 knew all three facts about St. Patrick.

   How many students knew only what he was famous for? How many students knew only his job? How many students knew only where he was born?

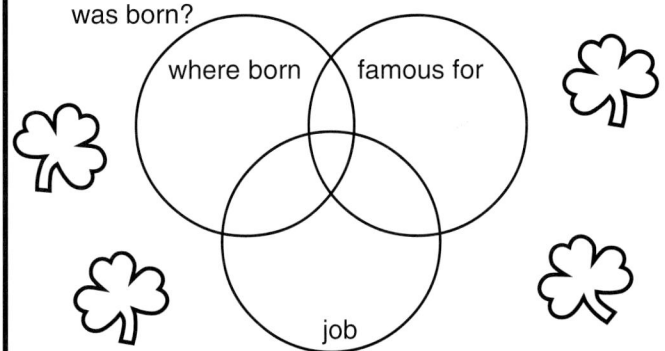

3. Murphy Middle School's softball team asked for support from local businesses at the beginning of the season. Seventeen businesses responded with the following: two donated uniforms only; four donated uniforms and equipment; three donated uniforms and refreshments; two donated equipment and refreshments; five donated equipment only; no one donated only refreshments; one donated all three.

   How many companies donated equipment? How many companies donated refreshments? How many companies donated uniforms?

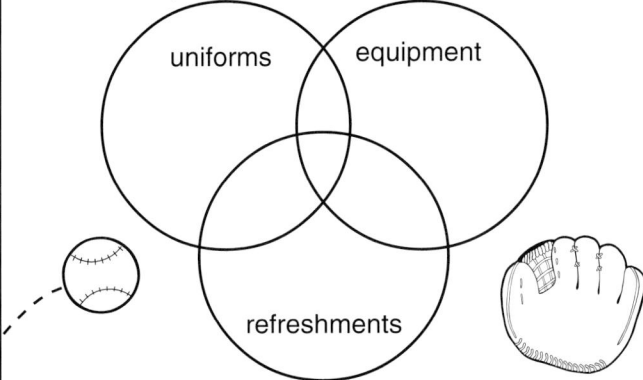

4. One hundred forty-four Americans were asked how they celebrate St. Patrick's Day. The results of the survey are as follows: 68 attend parades; 79 wear green; 53 attend a religious ceremony; 13 attend a religious ceremony and wear green; 9 attend a religious ceremony and parades; 26 attend parades and wear green; 4 do all three of these things.

   How many people only wear green? How many people only attend parades? How many people only attend religious ceremonies?

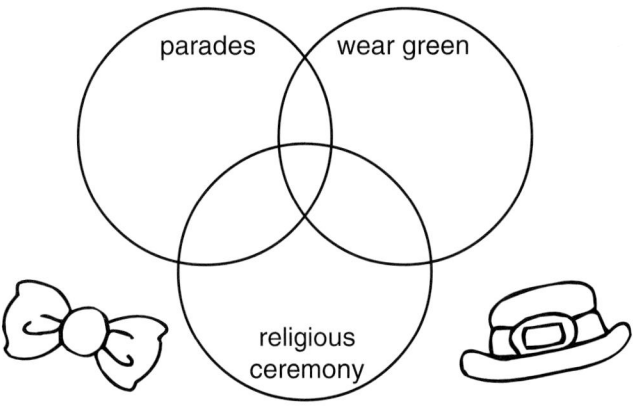

Bonus Box: Look again at problem 4 above. Suppose all those who wear green to a parade receive a free hat. If the hats are delivered in packages of 12, how many packages will be needed?

Top o' the Mornin' to Ye!
Activities to Explore Ireland—
The Land of Mist, Magic, and Mystique

Journey with your students to the Emerald Isle. Use the following activities to introduce your students to the people, land, and culture of Ireland.

by Caroline Chapman, Kelly Gooden, Thad McLaurin, Karen Richmond, and Irene Taylor

Over the Rainbow
Researching Irish culture

Legend says that if you are clever enough to catch a leprechaun, he might share his pot of gold. Have students fill their own pots of gold with facts about Ireland. Divide students into small groups. Give each group one 8" x 18" sheet of black paper, one 1" x 18" strip of black paper, one 9" x 12" sheet of green paper, scissors, a stapler, and tape. Have each group follow these directions to construct its pot of gold:

1. Make a series of two-inch cuts along one of the long sides of the large piece of black paper. Space the cuts 1 1/2 inches apart to resemble flaps as shown.
2. Form a cylinder by overlapping the two short ends of the paper. Secure the ends with tape.
3. Fold the flaps inward to form the bottom of the pot. Secure the flaps with tape.
4. Staple each end of the 1" x 18" strip to the inside of the pot to create a handle.
5. Decorate the outside of the pot with shamrocks cut from the green paper.

Direct each group to research five topics related to the culture of Ireland, such as family life, celebrations, folklore, foods, and crafts. Have each group create an artifact or information pamphlet to illustrate each topic. After each group presents its information to the class, place the group's items in its pot. Staple the pots to a bulletin board as shown.

Lucky, Lucky, Lucky Charms
Collecting and graphing data

One American cereal company has capitalized on the Irish legend of leprechauns to create Lucky Charms® cereal. The ads for this product encourage consumers to eat such marshmallow shapes as hearts, moons, and clover. Use this familiar cereal to review and improve each student's predicting, averaging, and graphing skills. Divide the class into groups of three. Give each group a plastic bowl filled with one cup of Lucky Charms®, a calculator, and one copy of page 58. Have each group follow the directions on page 58 to record a predicted and actual number of each marshmallow shape. Next, write the actual totals from each group on the board (see the illustration). Direct the students to find the sum (the class total) of each shape and divide that number by the number of groups to get an average number of shapes in the box of cereal.

In the next chart, have each group graph the totals for each marshmallow shape. Finally, guide each group to find the cost per ounce of the cereal. To do this, have each group divide the total cost of the cereal by the total number of ounces.

Marshmallow Shapes	Group Totals								Class Totals
	1	2	3	4	5	6	7	8	
Heart	10	3	12	6	5	14	9	18	77
Moon	6	8	2	5	9	6	6	7	49
Rainbow	11	10	6	14	8	2	8	9	68
Clover									
Pot of Gold									
Balloon									
Horseshoe									
Star									

A Taste of Ireland
Experiencing a cultural tradition

Mmm! Can you smell it? Nearly every block in Belfast—Northern Ireland's capital city—has a bakery. And nearly every bakery features Soda Farls (small, triangular cakes). They are quick and easy to make. So use the recipe below and treat your class to some Soda Farls and cups of hot tea during your study of Ireland.

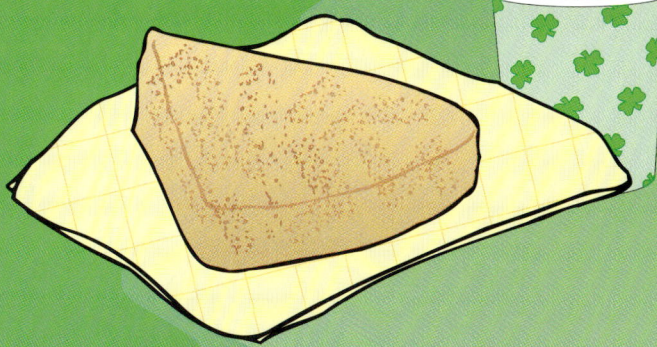

Ingredients:
1 c. all-purpose flour
1 c. cake flour
2 tsp. baking soda
1 tsp. salt
1 c. buttermilk

Directions:
Mix the dry ingredients together. Add buttermilk and stir to form a dough. Place the dough onto a floured board and knead gently. Divide the dough in half. Form each half into a circle about 10–12 inches in diameter; then cut each circle into quarters to form *farls*. In a skillet fry each farl in a "wee" bit of butter or margarine until browned (about 5–7 minutes on each side). You may need to set each farl on end to help cook the sides. This recipe makes eight farls. To conserve your ingredients, split one farl between two students or cut each farl into bite-size pieces.

Blarney Talk
Preparing and presenting a persuasive speech

Have you ever tried to talk your way out of doing something? If so, you have something in common with Cormac MacDermod—lord of Blarney Castle during the mid-fifteenth century. Queen Elizabeth I of England asked MacDermod to show his loyalty by giving away his castle. For many days he offered excuses to the queen until she finally declared that she'd heard enough of his "Blarney talk" and let him keep his castle. To this day, it is believed that anyone who kisses the Blarney stone, located in the south wall of Blarney Castle, will receive Cormac MacDermod's gift of persuasive talk.

Cover a shoebox with gray paper and label it "Blarney Box." On 3" x 5" index cards, write 10–15 topics for persuasive speeches—one per card—and place the cards in the box. Include such topics as "Why schools should stay closed on Saturdays," and "Why milkshakes should be served every day at lunch." Periodically during your study of Ireland, have a student pull a card from the box. Tell the student to imagine that he has just kissed the Blarney stone and is now "full of blarney." Give him five minutes to prepare and one minute to present a "Blarney Talk" in which he tries to persuade his classmates to support the card's topic.

An Irish Getaway
Researching a city, narrative writing

Pack your bags for a journey to the Emerald Isle. Have students check out a travel guide from the library, visit a travel agency, or write to the Irish Tourist Board or Embassy (see an almanac for an address). Duplicate page 59 for each student. Instruct the student to use her page along with tourist pamphlets, brochures, and travel books to plan a trip to Dublin, Ireland. Direct each student to plan the activities and expenses for each day of her trip by writing an itinerary. In addition, have each student write a fictional journal page for each day of the trip describing the places she visited and any interesting facts she learned. Allow students several days to complete the activity. Then let each student present her itinerary, expenses, and adventures to the rest of the class. Bon voyage!

Itinerary—Monday

Time	Activity	Cost
8:00	Pay for night's lodging at Inn	$90.00
9:00	Continental breakfast	$3.50
9:30	Taxi to Blarney Castle	$5.00
10:00	Tour of Blarney Castle	$1.00
11:30	Taxi back to Inn	$5.00
1:30	Lunch—Irish pizza	$9.00
2:00	Rest	
3:00	Walking tour of Dublin	$20.00
6:00	Dinner—Lobster	$28.00
	Monday's Expenses	$161.50

'Tis a Soft Day
Interpreting and graphing data

The climate in Ireland is surprisingly mild given its northern latitude. To help students compare temperature variations around Ireland, have them prepare temperature bar graphs for the cities of Dublin, Cork, and Belfast by using the information below. Also have students graph and compare the high, low, or average temperatures for each city.

After completing their graphs, have students discuss the ranges between the months with the highest and lowest temperatures. Based on their graphs, have students describe the climate for Ireland.

	Dublin		Cork		Belfast	
	High	Low	High	Low	High	Low
Jan.	47°F	34°F	49°F	36°F	43°F	36°F
Feb.	47°F	36°F	49°F	38°F	45°F	36°F
Mar.	50°F	38°F	52°F	40°F	49°F	38°F
Apr.	56°F	40°F	56°F	41°F	54°F	50°F
May	59°F	43°F	61°F	45°F	59°F	43°F
June	65°F	49°F	67°F	50°F	65°F	49°F
July	68°F	52°F	68°F	54°F	65°F	52°F
Aug.	67°F	52°F	68°F	54°F	65°F	52°F
Sept.	63°F	49°F	65°F	50°F	61°F	49°F
Oct.	58°F	43°F	58°F	45°F	56°F	45°F
Nov.	50°F	40°F	52°F	40°F	49°F	40°F
Dec.	47°F	38°F	49°F	38°F	45°F	38°F

Two Faces of Ireland
Researching countries, writing comparison paragraphs

The island of Ireland has two different and distinct faces. The Republic of Ireland, an independent nation, shares the Emerald Isle with Northern Ireland, a province of the United Kingdom. Duplicate page 60 for each group of three students. Instruct each group to research the differences and similarities between these two countries and record its findings on page 60. Then have each group use the information to write two paragraphs—one describing the similarities between The Republic of Ireland and Northern Ireland, and one describing the differences. Enlarge and copy the map of Ireland (page 60) onto green bulletin board paper. Instruct each group to write a final draft of its paragraphs on a green shamrock cutout. Post these cutouts around the map of Ireland for an attractive display.

Names _____ Math: predicting, graphing, and averaging skills

Lucky Hearts, Moons, and Stars

Add a little luck to your math and observation skills to get a handle on these lucky charms!

Part A:
1. Look at the bowl of cereal your teacher has given you. Without touching the cereal, predict how many of each marshmallow shape are in the bowl. Record your predictions in column A on the chart below.
2. Pour out the cereal and count each shape. Record those totals in column B.
3. Give the teacher the totals from column B to record on the board.
4. Using the information from the board, add up each group's totals for each shape. Record each class total in column C.
5. Divide each class total by the number of groups to get an average for each shape. Record that number in column D.

Marshmallow Shapes	A Prediction	B Actual Amount	C Class Total	D Average
Heart				
Moon				
Rainbow				
Clover				
Pot of Gold				
Balloon				
Horseshoe				
Star				

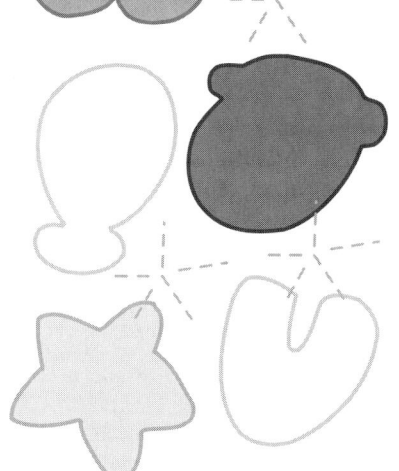

Part B: Use the information in the chart above to graph the total number of each type of marshmallow in one box of cereal.

Class Total of Marshmallows

Marshmallow Shapes: Heart, Moon, Rainbow, Clover, Pot of Gold, Balloon, Horseshoe, Star

Total Number of Marshmallows: 0 5 10 15 20 25 30 35 40 45 50 55 60 65 70 75 80 85 90 95 100

Part C:

Total Cost of Cereal $ _____ ÷ Total Ounces _____ oz. = Cost Per Ounce $ _____

©The Education Center, Inc. • MARCH • TEC208

Note to the teacher: Use with "Lucky, Lucky, Lucky Charms" on page 55. Provide each student group with one cup of cereal in a bowl and a calculator.

Name _____

Planning a trip

Pack Your Bags!

Student directions: Use the guidelines and information below to plan a trip to Dublin, Ireland.

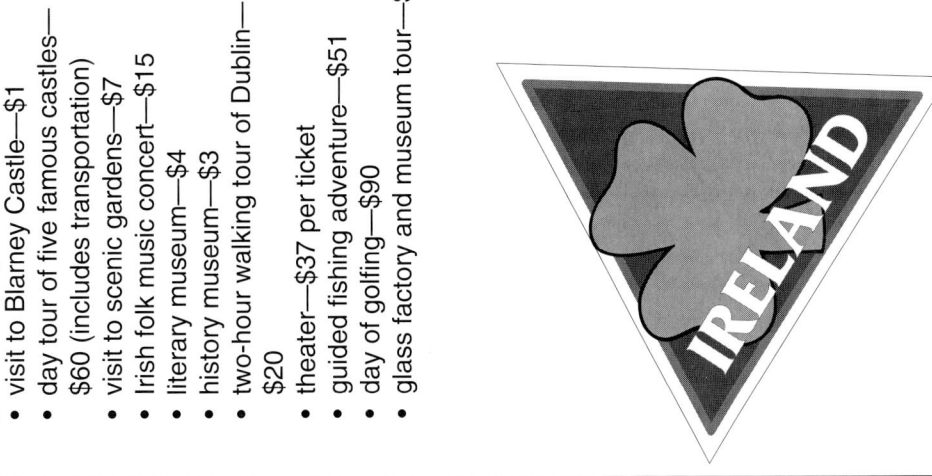

Guidelines:

1. You will arrive on a Saturday evening before dinner and leave the following Saturday morning after breakfast.
2. Your total budget is $3,000.
3. You must pay for:
   - at least three of the items listed under Pretrip Purchases
   - a round-trip plane ticket
   - a place to stay for seven nights
   - at least two meals each day
   - at least one new activity each day

Pretrip purchases:
- camera—$230
- walking shoes—$60
- umbrella—$17
- film—$38
- luggage—$373
- jacket—$45

Airline options:
- first class (round-trip) ticket—$890
- coach (round-trip) ticket—$540

Lodging options:
1. Dublin Castle Inn
   - suite—$180 per night
   - single—$90 per night
2. Shamrock Lodge
   - single—$50 per night
3. Cottage rental—$445 for seven nights

Food options:
- continental breakfast—$3.50 per day
- Irish stew—$5.50 per bowl
- salmon and creamed potatoes—$11.90
- shrimp and scallops—$18
- lobster—$28
- corned beef and cabbage—$9
- beef and creamed potatoes—$6.50
- soup with Irish soda bread—$2.50
- steak-and-kidney pie—$6
- Irish pizza—$9
- lamb in pastry—$28

Souvenir options:
- crystal vase from Waterford—$95
- handmade wool sweater—$110
- four-leaf-clover bookmark—$1.25
- Irish coffee mug—$25
- antique Irish ring—$240
- tweed suit—$189
- Irish flag—$19
- original painting of Irish countryside—$499

Sight-seeing options: (per person)
- visit to Blarney Castle—$1
- day tour of five famous castles—$60 (includes transportation)
- visit to scenic gardens—$7
- Irish folk music concert—$15
- literary museum—$4
- history museum—$3
- two-hour walking tour of Dublin—$20
- theater—$37 per ticket
- guided fishing adventure—$51
- day of golfing—$90
- glass factory and museum tour—$8

Transportation options: (all sights are approximately two miles from your hotel)
1. taxi—$5 one way, any destination
2. scooter rental—$60 per day
3. car rental
   - $150 per week (7 days)
   - $25 per day

Names _____ _____

Comparing and contrasting

Two Faces of Ireland

The Republic of Ireland and Northern Ireland share the Emerald Isle. As a group, research the two lands and use the space below to record the similarities and differences between them in such areas as government, economy, culture, and climate. Next, use this information to write two paragraphs—one describing the similarities between The Republic of Ireland and Northern Ireland, and one describing the differences.

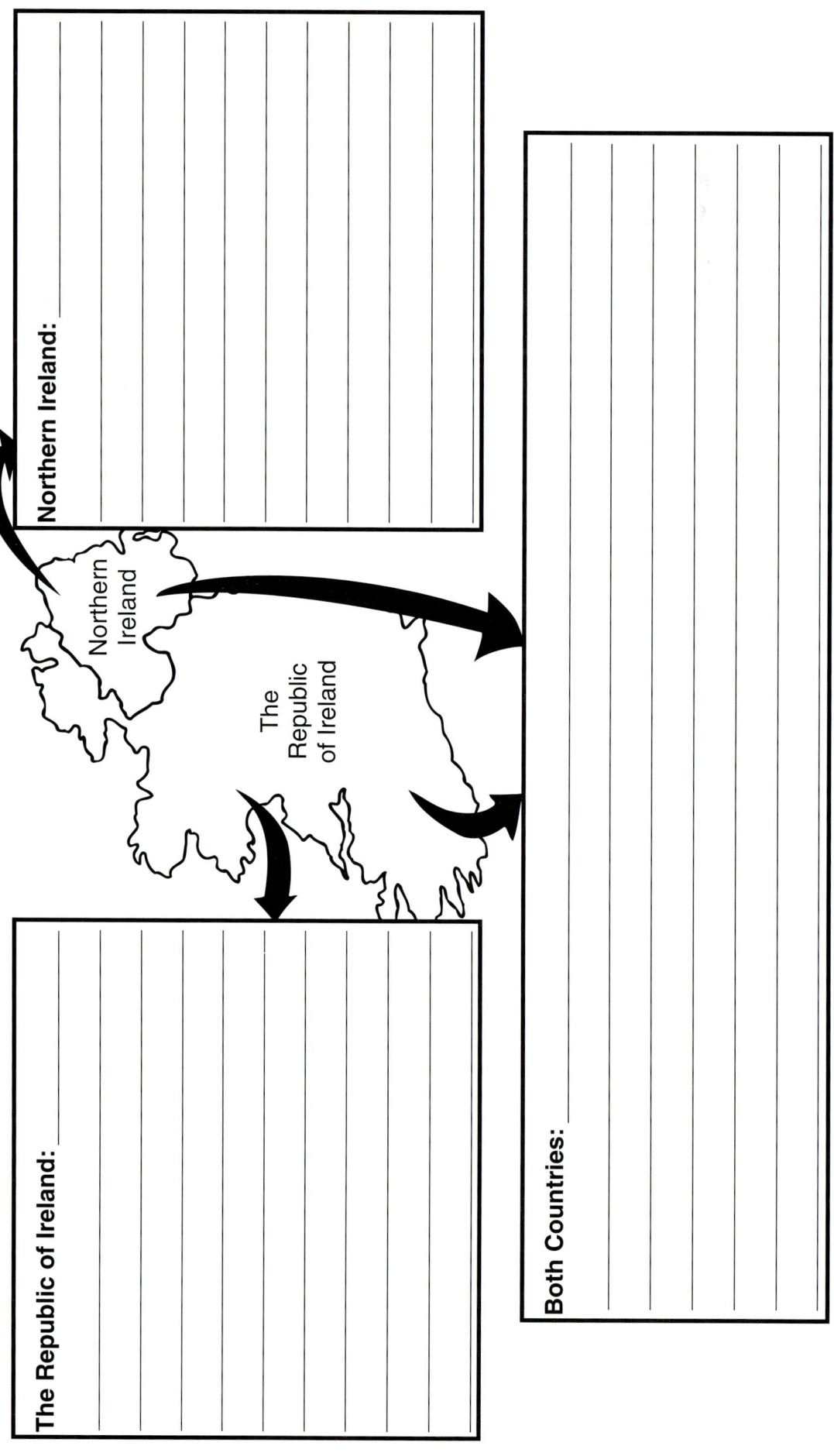

Note to the teacher: Duplicate this page for each group and use it with "Two Faces of Ireland" on page 57.

Name(s) _____ Logic puzzle

Four of a Kind

Tom, Patrick, Stephen, and Sean are very close friends who live in four different cities and come from four different families. They share many hobbies and interests. Use the clues below to match each boy's first name with his last name and hometown. Use an *X* to eliminate options, and use an *O* to indicate a match. After completing the chart, fill in the map below by writing the first and last name of each boy by his hometown.

	Dublin	Limerick	Kilkenny	Tipperary	McMurphy	McNamara	O'Leary	O'Mally
Tom								
Patrick								
Stephen								
Sean								
McMurphy				
McNamara				
O'Leary				
O'Mally				

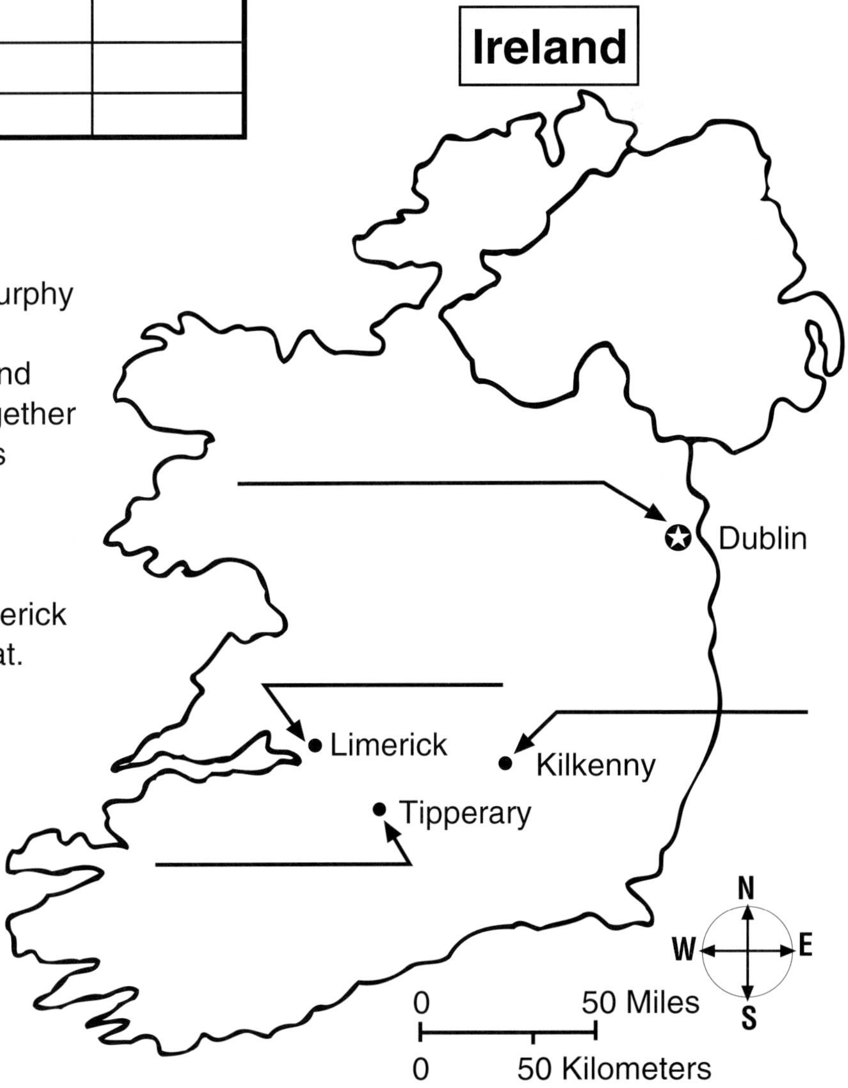

Clues:
1. Tom and O'Mally like to visit McMurphy in Tipperary.
2. Stephen, the boy from Limerick, and O'Leary all play Gaelic football together while the boy from Tipperary takes pictures.
3. Neither Sean nor O'Leary lives in Kilkenny.
4. Both Patrick and the boy from Limerick enjoy fishing on the Dubliner's boat.
5. McNamara lives in Kilkenny.
6. Sean's name is not McMurphy.
7. Tom has lived in Dublin all his life.

Ireland

(Map of Ireland showing Dublin, Limerick, Kilkenny, and Tipperary, with a scale of 50 Miles / 50 Kilometers and a compass rose)

Bonus Box: Use the map of Ireland to calculate the distance that each boy lives from Ireland's capital city.

On Your Mark, Get Set, GROW!

What are some of the most important organisms on Earth? GREEN PLANTS! Plants provide oxygen for the atmosphere and at the same time clean up pollutants in the air such as carbon dioxide. What better month than March—with its first day of spring—to explore the power of plants!

by Maureen Winkler, Lorraine Brandt, and Thad McLaurin

Which Way Do I Grow?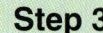
Conducting an experiment, understanding geotropism

Do seeds know which way is up and which way is down? To find out, enlist student volunteers to help you conduct the following experiment.

Supplies: glass jar with a screw lid, 6 paper towels, water, 2 green bean seeds soaked in water overnight

Directions:
Step 1: Roll up six paper towels and place them in the glass jar.
Step 2: Moisten the paper towels with water.
Step 3: Insert two bean seeds between the paper towels and the glass so that each seed is visible from the outside of the jar as shown.
Step 4: Place the jar in a warm, sunny area. In about three days, observe the roots beginning to grow down from the seeds as shown. Keep the paper towels moist.
Step 5: When the roots are about one inch long and a shoot begins to push out of the top of the bean, screw the lid on tight and turn the jar upside down.
Step 6: Observe and record the growth of the roots and the shoots.

After three or four days, the roots turn and grow downward in a positive response to gravity. Meanwhile, the stems turn and grow upward in a negative response to gravity. This built-in growth response in plants is *called* geotropism.

Step 3

Step 4
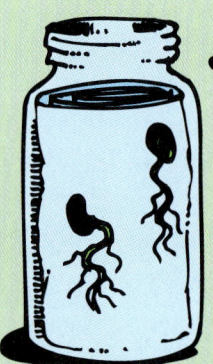

Results
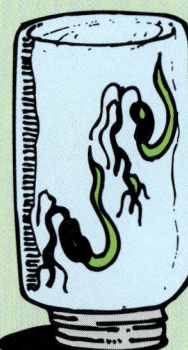

Germination Determination
Conducting an experiment, understanding germination

How do the seasons affect seed germination? Have each student predict how cold and warm weather affect germination. After recording their predictions, recruit student volunteers to help complete the following experiment:

Materials: 2 copies of page 71, refrigerator, 2 cookie sheets, roll of paper towels, water spray bottle, seeds—corn, lettuce, green bean, green pea, broccoli, radish, and sunflower

Procedure:
1. Place four layers of paper towels on each cookie sheet and spray them with water.
2. Place three of each kind of seed on top of the paper towels.
3. Top the seeds with four more layers of paper towels and spray them with water.
4. Store one cookie sheet in a warm, dark location and the other sheet in a refrigerator.
5. Place a copy of page 71 near each cookie sheet.
6. Each day for 15 days, spray the towels to keep them moist and then record any changes or growth of the seeds.

Follow-up discussion questions:
- Which class predictions were correct?
- Why is it important to plant seeds at the appropriate time of year?
- Are there any seeds that could be planted in the fall or winter? If so, which ones?

The seeds stored in the dark germinate and begin to grow; however, they need light to continue growing. The refrigerated seeds do not germinate. They need warmth to do so.

The Write Time
Critical thinking, writing for a purpose

Challenge your students each day with a critical-thinking question on the topic of plants and their awesome power. Give each student about 15 minutes to respond in writing. After time is called, let each student share his response. Then have students discuss the various answers.

Suggested topics/questions:
- What are some uses of plants?
- Why are plants so important to our existence?
- Besides providing food, why are plants so vital to animal survival?
- What do trees do for the environment?
- How do plants affect your everyday life?
- How does recycling paper products help plants?
- Is there such a thing as a carnivorous plant?
- Often two plants are crossbred to create a new plant. What two plants would you crossbreed and why?

HONEY, I BLEW UP THE PLANTS
Observing plants, writing for a purpose

Allow your students to take a closer look at the plants they pass by each day. Supply each student with a magnifying glass, two sheets of notebook paper, and a pencil; then take the class outside. Inform each student that he will be using the following KWL technique to observe each plant:

- **K**—Write down what you **know** about the plant.
- **W**—Write down what you **want** to learn about the plant.
- **L**—Write down what you **learned** about the plant after completing your examination.

Instruct each student to select a plant to examine using the magnifying glass. Suggest such plants as grasses, evergreens, or other spring-blooming plants that are emerging in your schoolyard. Instruct the student to observe the plant in its location and not to pick the plant or damage it. Have each student use the KWL method to record his observations on the first sheet of notebook paper and then illustrate his plant on the second sheet. Return to the classroom and have each student present his observations and illustration. Post these findings around the classroom for the duration of your plants unit.

PLANT POWER
Understanding the connection between organisms and the environment, researching plants

The power of plant survival can be seen from the extreme conditions of the driest desert to the lush, humid, tropical rain forests. Help students comprehend the vast diversity of the plant world with the following activity. Divide students into ten groups. Have each group research plants that are unique to one of the ten major land biomes. Give each group one piece of white poster board, markers, and crayons. After each group has collected its research, instruct it to illustrate the plants found in its biome. Direct each group to include a title, the biome's basic location, and a brief description of each plant on the poster. Have each group present its work to the class. Display the posters in the classroom or in the hallway.

Major Land Biomes
- tundra
- boreal forest or taiga forest
- temperate coniferous forest
- temperate deciduous forest
- chaparral
- desert
- grassland
- savanna
- tropical seasonal forest
- tropical rain forest

THANK YOU, TREES
Understanding the connection between organisms and the environment, writing for a purpose

Nothing can replace trees—that's why they are so important to the environment. Help students understand the importance of trees by reading *The Giving Tree* by Shel Silverstein. Have students brainstorm a list of products made from trees. Then astound the class by telling them that more than 5,000 products and by-products come from trees. Add to the list some of the more unusual products, such as bleach, carpet, cattle feed, makeup, and soap.

Create a bulletin board by having each student bring in one item (or a picture of the item) made from tree products. Also instruct each student to write a short thank-you note to a tree for helping to make the product possible. Cut out a large tree shape from green and brown paper and center it on a bulletin board. Post each student's product and thank-you note on the tree. Title the board "Thank You, Trees." Take time to let each student share his product and thank-you note with the class.

TAKE A CLOSER LOOK
Classifying plants

Botanists divide flowering plants into two classes—*monocotyledons* (monocots) and *dicotyledons* (dicots). The first sprout or *cotyledon* of a monocot has only one leaf—called the seed leaf. A dicot has two seed leaves. Most monocots have leaves with parallel veins and flower petals in multiples of three. Dicots, however, have leaves with veins that run in a netlike pattern and flower petals in multiples of four or five. If possible, take your class outside to collect flowering plants from the area around your school, or request that your local plant store or nursery donate or loan a variety of flowering plants. Supplement the collection with pictures and illustrations. Number 10–15 plants and pictures and display them on tables around the classroom. Make one copy of page 73 for each student. Instruct her to use the information on the reproducible to help her classify each plant as a monocot or a dicot. After each student has completed the task, hold up the first plant and have a student volunteer tell whether it's a monocot or a dicot and why. Then continue with the second plant and so on until all the plants have been correctly identified.

WHAT ARE FUNGI?
Understanding plant reproduction, observing plant matter

Fungi are so odd that many botanists do not consider them to be plants. Unlike plants, fungi do not make seeds, they contain no chlorophyll, and they cannot make their own food. So, how do they grow? Fungi produce millions of microscopic spores that are carried by the wind. The spores land on the soil and form more fungi by absorbing food from plants and animals.

Have students make spore prints to see how fungi such as mushrooms release spores. Divide students into pairs. Give each pair one large edible mushroom cap and one sheet of white paper. Have each pair examine the bat-shaped structures containing the spore cells on the underside of its mushroom cap. Instruct each pair to place the flat side of its mushroom cap on the white paper. Store the mushroom caps on an undisturbed table for three days. Then have each pair lift its mushroom off the paper. The pair will observe that rings of dark powder have formed. Explain to students that the powder is made of spores. Ask the students what might happen if the wind carried the spores outside.

WE CAN EAT THAT?
Identifying plant products, identifying the structure of a plant

Many different plant parts can be used as food, drink, or even medicine. For example, we eat the stems of asparagus, the roots of carrots and beets, and the leaves of cabbage and spinach. Divide students into groups of two or three to create posters illustrating the numerous foods that come from plants. Give each group one large piece of white poster board, glue, scissors, markers, and several old magazines. Instruct each group to sketch a large plant—complete with roots, stems, and leaves—on its board. Then have each group search the magazines for pictures of foods. Instruct each group to cut out the pictures and then glue them beside the appropriate parts of the plant. Challenge each group to identify some unusual edible plant parts. For example, nasturtium flowers, marigolds, and rose petals make an attractive and tasty addition to a tossed salad. Display the posters around the classroom; then have each group share the different foods on its poster.

The ABCs of Plants
Researching types of plants, writing for a purpose

Do your students know their ABCs? To find out, have students work in pairs to create alphabet flip books. Stock the classroom with reference materials on plants, old magazines, glue, scissors, crayons, and markers. Provide each pair with 30 lined 4" x 6" index cards and a copy of page 74. Direct each pair to research one plant for each letter of the alphabet, recording each plant's information on a card as illustrated on page 74. Have each pair add an illustration on the back of each card. Then instruct the pair to use the remaining cards to create a front and back cover, a title page, and an "About the Authors" page. Assemble each book by hole-punching two holes along the left side of each card. Line up the cards in order and secure both holes with metal rings. Encourage students to check out each other's books to share with their families.

Beauty Is Only Petal Deep!
Understanding plant reproduction, creating a model

Most flowers are beautiful, but some look more flamboyant or smell better than others. Why? The answer has to do with pollination—the process by which pollen is transported from male flower parts to female flower parts. Different plants rely on different methods to transport pollen. The more flamboyant flowers tempt animals with their bright colors and sweet smells. When these animals and insects visit a flower, they pick up pollen and carry it to the next flower. Less attractive flowers that lack petals and sepals rely on the wind to transport pollen.

Have students identify flowers that use these methods of pollination. Then have each student create a three-dimensional model of a flower. Provide a supply of materials such as tissue paper, colored paper, pipe cleaners, toothpicks, markers, crayons, glue, scissors, and glitter. Instruct each student to include the following flower parts on his model: petals, sepals, pistil, and stamens. Then have each student write a brief description of the flower to place by his model. Schedule a time for each student to present his model and explain how the flower is pollinated. Display the models in the classroom or media center.

SPROUTS, ANYONE?
Conducting an experiment

Been to a salad bar lately? Then you've probably eaten sprouts. Test your students' knowledge of sprouts and how we get them. Display some sprouts on a plate and ask how many of your students have eaten sprouts in a salad. Then ask if anyone knows where sprouts come from and how they are made. List the responses on the board. Next, inform the students that the class is going to grow its own sprouts. Obtain some untreated alfalfa seeds, bean seeds, radish seeds, green lentils, or a combination of seeds from your health-food store. Do not use garden seeds as they may be treated with a poison! Enlist student volunteers to help with the following experiment.

Step 1: Place the seeds in a glass jar. Cover the seeds with cold water and soak them overnight.
Step 2: The following day, place the seeds in a colander or strainer and rinse them with cold water. Then return the seeds to the jar. Use a hammer and nail to punch holes in the lid; then screw it onto the jar. Keep the jar in a dark, warm place.
Step 3: Repeat the rinsing procedure each morning and afternoon. In five days the sprouts are ready to eat.

Encourage each student to sample the sprouts in a salad, or have parent volunteers stir-fry the sprouts in oil with other garden vegetables. Bon appetit!

BLOOMING POETRY
Writing haiku poems

Inspire students to combine nature and poetry with the following activity. Have each student write a haiku about a favorite flower on an unlined 4" x 6" index card. A haiku is a form of Japanese poetry that consists of three nonrhyming lines and usually describes some aspect of nature. The first line of a haiku contains five syllables, the second line contains seven syllables, and the third line contains five syllables.

To illustrate each poem, have each student rummage through old magazines to find a picture of his favorite flower. Give each student a piece of white paper, scissors, glue, and crayons. Have each student cut his magazine picture in half, then glue one half to the white sheet of paper, leaving space where the missing half would have gone. Instruct each student to use crayons to complete the missing half of the picture. Then have each student glue his index card and illustration to a piece of colored construction paper. Post the poems on a bulletin board with the title "Blooming Poetry" cut from floral wallpaper.

You Are What You Mow
Conducting an experiment

Have you ever eaten grass seed for breakfast? You sure have! Rice, corn, oats, and wheat are in the cereal-grass family. Bring out the artist in each student with the following grass-seed sculptures. Purchase or gather the following items: a one-pound bag of grass seed from a lawn-and-garden center, one inexpensive sponge for each student, several cookie sheets, scissors, and a spray bottle. Instruct each student to cut his sponge into an unusual shape. Have each student dip his sponge in a bucket of water, then squeeze out any excess water. Direct each student to place his sponge on a cookie sheet and sprinkle the sponge with grass seeds. Set the trays in a sunny area of the room. Use the spray bottle to moisten the sponges each day. In four or five days, the sculptures will start to come alive with sprouts.

"Chef Soil-Ardee"
Conducting an experiment

Put those leftover food scraps from your students' lunches to good use with the following activity. Collect two cups of nonmeat food scraps such as bread, fruits, and vegetables from your students at the end of a lunch period. Place the scraps in a plastic, zippered freezer bag and store the bag in the refrigerator. Tell your students the scraps will be used to make *compost*. Explain that compost is a mixture of decayed organic matter used as a fertilizer. Enlist several student volunteers to make the compost recipe below.

Materials:
- two cups of foods scraps (no meat or oil)
- one cup of garden soil (not potting soil)
- one gallon-size, plastic zippered freezer bag
- water

Compost recipe:
Step 1: Combine the garden soil, the food scraps, and a little water in the freezer bag.
Step 2: Blow some air into bag; then close the bag and shake well.
Step 3: Shake the bag once a day. At the end of each week, add some fresh air to the bag. The soil will be turned into compost in about two weeks.
Step 4: Mix the compost with two cups of garden soil in a planter or flowerpot. Then plant some seeds or rooted plants in the compost mixture and watch them grow!

Plant the Seeds of Curiosity
Conducting an experiment, understanding conditions necessary for plant growth

Under what conditions do plants grow best? Help students answer this question by dividing them into four teams to complete the four experiments below. Purchase eight small, inexpensive plants (all the same species) from a local greenhouse. Duplicate the experiments below; then cut along the dotted lines. Give each team the appropriate set of directions. Conduct the experiments over a period of ten school days. Conclude by having each team present its data. Then have the class determine which set of conditions were best for plant growth.

Materials for each team:
- copy of page 72
- 2 small, healthy potted plants of the same species
- ruler, red marker, blue marker
- 1/4-cup measure
- plant food (Team C only)
- water

Team A
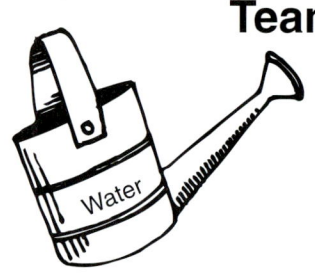

Goal: Compare the growth of a well-watered plant to the growth of a plant that receives no water.
Procedure:
- Label one plant "A" and one plant "B." Both plants receive sunlight.
- Give plant "A" 1/4 cup of water each day. Do not water plant "B."
- Measure and record the height of both plants each day.

©The Education Center, Inc. • *MARCH* • TEC208

Team B
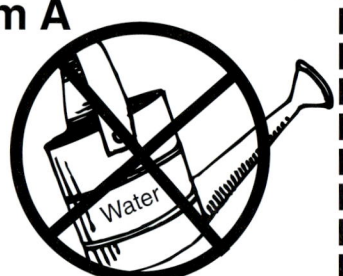

Goal: Compare the growth of a plant receiving sunlight to the growth of a plant kept in darkness.
Procedure:
- Label one plant "A" and one plant "B."
- Place plant "A" in full sunlight. Place plant "B" in complete darkness.
- Give both plants 1/4 cup of water each day.
- Measure and record the height of both plants each day.

©The Education Center, Inc. • *MARCH* • TEC208

Team C

Goal: Compare the growth of a plant receiving water and plant food to the growth of a plant receiving only water.
Procedure:
- Label one plant "A" and one plant "B." Both plants receive sunlight.
- Give plant "A" water and plant food on the first day. Give plant "B" only water the first day. On each of the remaining days, give both plants 1/4 cup of plain water.
- Measure and record the height of both plants each day.

©The Education Center, Inc. • *MARCH* • TEC208

Team D

Goal: Compare the growth of a plant that is talked to each day to the growth of a plant that is not talked to at all.
Procedure:
- Label one plant "A" and one plant "B." Both plants receive sunlight.
- Give both plants 1/4 cup of water each day.
- Talk to plant "A" in a nice, soothing voice each day. Do not talk to plant "B" at all.
- Measure and record the height of both plants each day.

©The Education Center, Inc. • *MARCH* • TEC208

Note to the teacher: Duplicate the four science activities above; then cut apart each experiment along the dotted lines. Use with "Plant the Seeds of Curiosity" at the top of this page and "Plotted Plants" on page 72.

Germination Determination
Observation Sheet

Directions: Use the codes below the chart to record each daily observation.

Location of cookie tray: _____

Seeds	Day 1	Day 2	Day 3	Day 4	Day 5	Day 6	Day 7	Day 8	Day 9	Day 10	Day 11	Day 12	Day 13	Day 14	Day 15
Corn															
Lettuce															
Green Bean															
Green Pea															
Broccoli															
Radish															
Sunflower															

NC = No change from yesterday.
G = The seeds have begun to sprout (germinate).
CG = The seeds continue to grow.
M = The seeds are getting moldy.
D = The seeds are drying up.

©The Education Center, Inc. • *MARCH* • TEC208

Note to the teacher: Duplicate two copies of this page to use with "Germination Determination" on page 63.

Team Members _____ *Graphing*

"Plotted" Plants

1. Before conducting the experiment, predict what will happen to each plant.

   Plant "A": _____
   _____

   Plant "B": _____
   _____

2. Plot the daily growth of each plant on the bar graph below. Use a red marker for plant "A" and a blue marker for plant "B."

Growth Chart

Height in Inches	A	B	A	B	A	B	A	B	A	B	A	B	A	B	A	B	A	B	A	B
15																				
14																				
13																				
12																				
11																				
10																				
9																				
8																				
7																				
6																				
5																				
4																				
3																				
2																				
1																				
0																				
	Day 1		Day 2		Day 3		Day 4		Day 5		Day 6		Day 7		Day 8		Day 9		Day 10	

3. Based on your data, what can you conclude from your team's experiment? _____
_____

©The Education Center, Inc. • MARCH • TEC208

Note to the teacher: Use with "Plant the Seeds of Curiosity" on page 70.

Name _____   *Classifying*

TAKE A CLOSER LOOK
(Classifying Flowering Plants as Monocots or Dicots)

Flowering plants are classified as *monocots* or *dicots*. Study the chart below to learn the characteristics of each.

Examine each numbered plant or picture displayed. Use the information in the chart to help you classify each plant as either a monocot or a dicot. Beginning with the column titled "Leaf Vein Pattern," check off each category that applies to each plant. Be prepare to explain why you classified each plant as a monocot or a dicot.

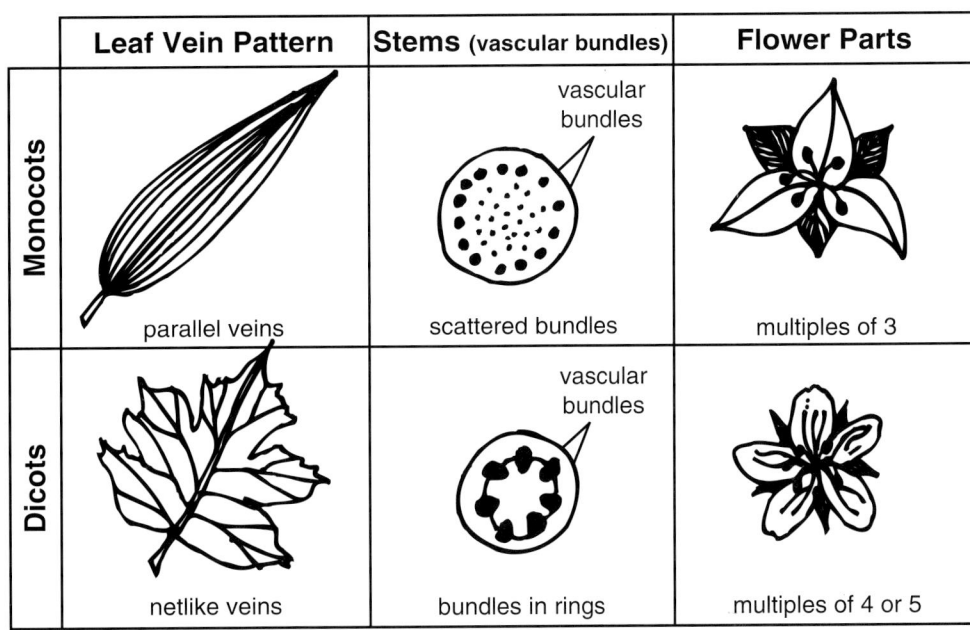

Plant (Number & Name)	Leaf Vein Pattern		Stems (vascular bundles)		Flower Parts		Classification	
	Parallel veins	Netlike veins	Scattered	Rings	Multiples of 3	Multiples of 4 or 5	Dicot	Monocot
1.								
2.								
3.								
4.								
5.								
6.								
7.								
8.								
9.								
10.								
11.								
12.								
13.								
14.								
15.								

©The Education Center, Inc. • MARCH • TEC208

Note to the teacher: Duplicate this page for each student to use with "Take a Closer Look" on page 65.

Names _____ Research organization

ALPHABET FLIP BOOK PLANNING SHEET

Use this page to help you assign duties, gather information, and assemble your book.

Authors' names: _____

Title of book: _____

Responsibilities: (Decide who is going to research and illustrate each plant.)

• Author 1 (_____): _____
                name

• Author 2 (_____): _____
                name

Sample Card:

Page number: 3
Letter: A
Common name: Aster
Scientific name: A. novac angliae
Interesting facts: Most asters are perennials, which means they live more than two years, but some are annuals and die after one growing season. Asters are hard to grow from seed.
Source: The World Book Multimedia Encyclopedia™

Arrange your book in this order:
- Cover page (title and illustration)
- Title page (title, authors' names, and copyright)
- 26 pages (one page, front and back, for each letter of the alphabet)
- Authors' page (background information on each author)
- Back cover page (brief description of the book and an illustration)

Name _____

Parent/student activity

How Does Your Garden Grow?

Start your own garden from seed at home. Below are a list of supplies and directions that you and your parents can use to begin your own vegetable or flower garden.

Supplies:

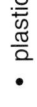

- seed tray or plastic tray with holes poked in the bottom for each type of seed
- seed tray with no holes for each type of seed
- potting soil
- flower or vegetable seeds
- water
- plastic wrap

Directions:

Step 1: Cover a table or flat surface with several layers of newspaper.

Step 2: Set each tray with holes inside a tray with no holes for drainage.

Step 3: Fill the top tray with potting soil. Then pour water on the soil until it is thoroughly saturated.

Step 4: Sprinkle seeds on the soil.

Step 5: Cover seeds with a thin layer of potting soil.

Step 6: Cover each tray with plastic wrap.

Step 7: Place the trays in a warm, dark place. Don't water until germination takes place.

Step 8: When the seedlings touch the plastic wrap, remove the wrap and place the trays in a sunny, warm place.

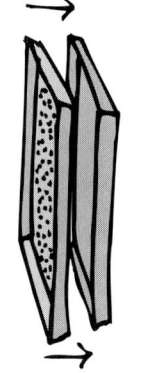
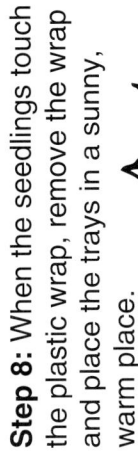

Step 9: When the seedlings are a few inches tall, transplant them to pots or to an outside garden spot.

Step 10: Be sure to water your garden when the soil becomes dry.

Note to the teacher: Duplicate this page for each student. Encourage each student to complete the activity at home with his or her parents.

Incredible Eggs

Eggs have served a variety of purposes throughout history, ranging from food source to religious symbol. In many cultures, the egg is recognized as a symbol of new life and rebirth. If you're looking for a way to breathe some new life into your lessons and get into the swing of spring, the activities in this unit are "eggs-actly" what you need!

by Stephanie Willett-Smith

Grade-A Bulletin Board
Motivating students

The United States Department of Agriculture classifies eggs with a grade of AA, A, or B depending on their quality. Now you can show all of your students that you think their writing is Grade A with this eye-catching bulletin board. Enlarge the chicken on page 81. Cut 1" x 6" strips of brown construction paper. Overlap the strips and staple them to your bulletin board to make a large nest. Mount your students' writings on egg-shaped pieces of construction paper; then display the eggs in and around the nest. Each student will be thrilled to have his best work displayed for everyone to see.

New Beginnings Poetry Tree
Making a personal connection, writing poetry

Looking for a way to perk up that poetry lesson? If so, you'll want to try this fun seasonal activity. Begin by discussing how an egg represents a new beginning in life. After all, eggs are the means by which new life is created. Have your students brainstorm new beginnings they have experienced and discuss what these new beginnings have meant in their lives. Offer the following suggestions:
- the first day of school
- learning to ride a bike
- meeting someone new
- learning to read
- moving to a new town

Have each student select one new beginning as a topic for a short poem. Provide each student with a copy of page 81 on which to record her poem. Have each student follow the directions on the page to create a fold-out egg.

Point out to your students that in the past, farmers hung eggs from trees with the hope that abundant harvests would follow. You can make a similar egg tree to display the poetry eggs. Use a good-sized branch that has fallen from a tree. Spray-paint it and anchor it in a coffee can with sand or gravel. Attach your students' poetry eggs to the branches. The result will be an attractive display that offers a fun, easy way to promote poetry in your class.

"Egg-ceptional" Vocabulary Review Center
Reviewing vocabulary

Your students will scramble to get to this easy-to-make center! Fill some plastic eggs with strips of paper listing vocabulary words from the novel or story you are currently reading. Place the vocabulary eggs, along with a master list of vocabulary words and definitions, in the basket for small groups of students to use during free time.

To play, a student selects an egg from the basket, reads the vocabulary word it contains, and defines the word orally. Another student then checks to see if the correct definition was given. If the word is defined correctly, the student holds on to the egg as a point marker. If the student is unable to define the word, he puts the word strip back in the plastic egg and returns it to the basket. Students continue taking turns until all the eggs are gone; then each player totals up his points by counting the eggs he won.

The "Eggs-traordinary" Egg
Conducting an experiment to gain scientific information

Conduct this simple investigation to expose students to the scientific process and familiarize them with the parts of an egg. Duplicate page 82 for each student. Bring in a nonmetal mixing bowl.

Divide your class into groups of three. Give each group one fresh egg, two paper towels, three craft sticks, and a disposable soup bowl. Review the directions on page 82. Remind students to avoid cracking the yolks as they examine the eggs. Demonstrate how to crack an egg on the side of the mixing bowl. Then proceed around to each group and allow one student to crack his group's egg on the side of the mixing bowl. Have each group follow the step-by-step procedure on page 82 to investigate the parts of its egg. Instruct each student to wash his hands after Steps 2, 4, 6, and 8.

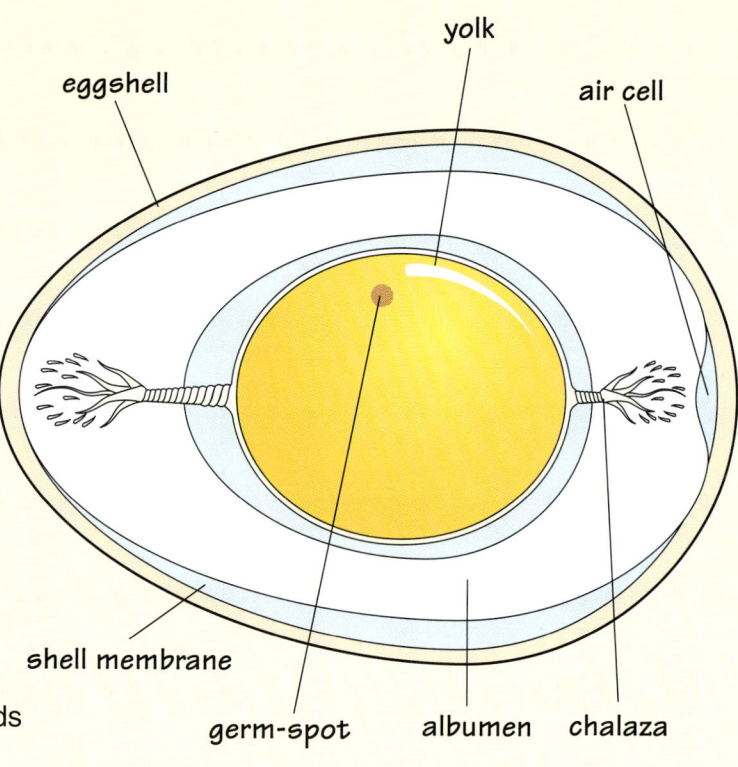

Helpful egg information:

The egg is made up of four main parts: the shell, *the* shell membrane, *the* albumen (*or* egg white), *and the* yolk. *The shell membrane is actually two thin, white membranes—the inner membrane and the outer membrane—that lie very close together. The* air cell *is located at the large end of the egg and is formed after the egg is laid. As the egg cools and contracts, a cell is formed between the inner and outer shell membranes. The* chalazas *are thick, white, ropelike structures at each end of the yolk that anchor the yolk but let it turn easily so that it is not damaged. Located on the yolk is a small, pinhead-sized spot that is lighter than the rest of the yolk. This is the* germ-spot *that will later develop into an embryo.*

Pass-the-Egg Relay Game
Reviewing spelling words

Want to get your students really "egg-cited" about spelling? Use this fun relay to review the spelling words you are currently studying.

Divide your class into small groups and assign a student facilitator in each group. Give each facilitator a plastic Easter egg and a spelling word list. Have him start the game by giving the egg to the first player in the group and then calling out the first word on the spelling list to that player. If the word is spelled correctly, have the player pass the egg to the next person in the group. Direct the facilitator to continue by calling the next word on the list. If a word is spelled incorrectly, instruct the player to pass the egg but allow the next student to try and spell the word correctly.

Have each group continue to pass its egg and spell the words until the list is finished. Then instruct the player who is holding the egg to bring it to the teacher while the other group members cluck like chickens to signify that the group is finished. The first group to finish its list and turn in its egg wins the spelling relay.

"Eggs-tra, Eggs-tra," Read All About It!
Writing for a purpose

Try a new approach for this month's class newsletter. Assign students to report on various topics of interest around your school, such as:

- What's Hatching?—recent activities
- "Egg-ceptional" Students—student achievements both in and out of school
- "Eggs-traordinary" Writing—students' writings
- "Eggs-press" Yourself—an editorial column
- "Dear Jen, Advice Hen"—an advice column
- "Egg-cellent" Reading—a book-review section

Make the final copy of the newsletter egg-shaped. Use the design of a cracked egg and cut the eggshell into several smaller sections. Give a section of the egg to each student to use for recording her article. Put all of the finished articles back together in the original egg shape to form the "Egg-ceptional" Newsletter.

Duplicate the newsletter and have students share it with other classes. Also be sure to send a copy home with each student.

Eggs, Eggs, Everywhere!
Researching eggs

Eggs have long been a part of the human diet. They also have many other uses that are not as well-known. Use the following activities to explore the various uses of the egg:

- Have your students work in small groups to generate lists of foods that contain eggs. On a large, egg-shaped piece of paper, combine all of the smaller lists into one master list. Continue to add to the list as students discover additional foods that contain eggs.
- Have students bring in the ingredient lists of products that contain eggs. Add these products to the list of egg-containing foods.
- Have students research the nutritive value of eggs. Make a two-column chart and categorize both the positive and negative points. Some positives: Eggs are a good source of protein, riboflavin, niacin, iron, phosphorus, and vitamins A, D, B3, B12, and E. Negatives: Eggs contain cholesterol and fat which can lead to heart disease.
- Have your students research other uses for the egg besides food—such as in some vaccines, shampoo, makeup, paint, ink, adhesives, and animal feed.
- To find out more about eggs, have your students write letters to the American Egg Board, 1460 Renaissance Drive, Park Ridge, IL 60068.

Recycling Egg Cartons
Planting and growing flowers

Egg cartons are used to transport eggs safely from one point to another. Now you can use them to help beautify your school just in time for Earth Day! Have your students save empty Styrofoam® egg cartons and clean eggshells for this project. You'll need to provide potting soil, flower seeds, toothpicks, and 1/2" x 2" paper strips. Select hardy flower seeds that are known to flourish in your region. Marigolds and zinnias work well in many areas. Give each student an egg carton, the materials listed above, and the following instructions:

1. Cut the top off each egg carton and set it aside.
2. Poke a small hole in the bottom of each section of the egg carton.
3. Place the lid under the egg carton to serve as a water collection tray.
4. Put a layer of crushed eggshells in the bottom of each of the twelve sections, followed by a layer of potting soil.
5. Place two to three seeds in each section and cover them with a thin layer of soil.
6. Make labels for the different flowers you plant, using toothpicks and strips of paper.
7. Water the seeds and place them in a well-lit area.

Have each student track the growth of his plants. When the seedlings reach a height of two inches, show each student how to transplant them into larger containers. Yogurt containers and foam cups work well for transplanting. When the weather warms, plant the flowers in various spots around your school. Everyone will appreciate your efforts to make the school a more beautiful place.

Egg-Hunt Review Game
Reviewing concepts and skills

Hunting for a fun way to review concepts? Try this exciting review game to reinforce any skills you are currently working on in class. You'll need some individually wrapped, egg-shaped chocolates; two clear plastic cups; and several egg-shaped cutouts. (Die-cut eggs are perfect.) Record each key term or concept on a paper egg.

Attach the paper eggs to the chalkboard with masking tape. Divide the class into two teams and place a plastic cup by each team. Have the first person on each team come to the chalkboard. Ask those two students a question. Award a piece of candy to the first student to find the egg with the correct answer. Have him place the candy in his team's plastic cup and tap the next player on his team to go to the board.

Continue play until you feel the concepts have been satisfactorily reviewed. Once the review session is over, have each team divide up its candy equally and return the extras to you. What a tasty way to review important concepts!

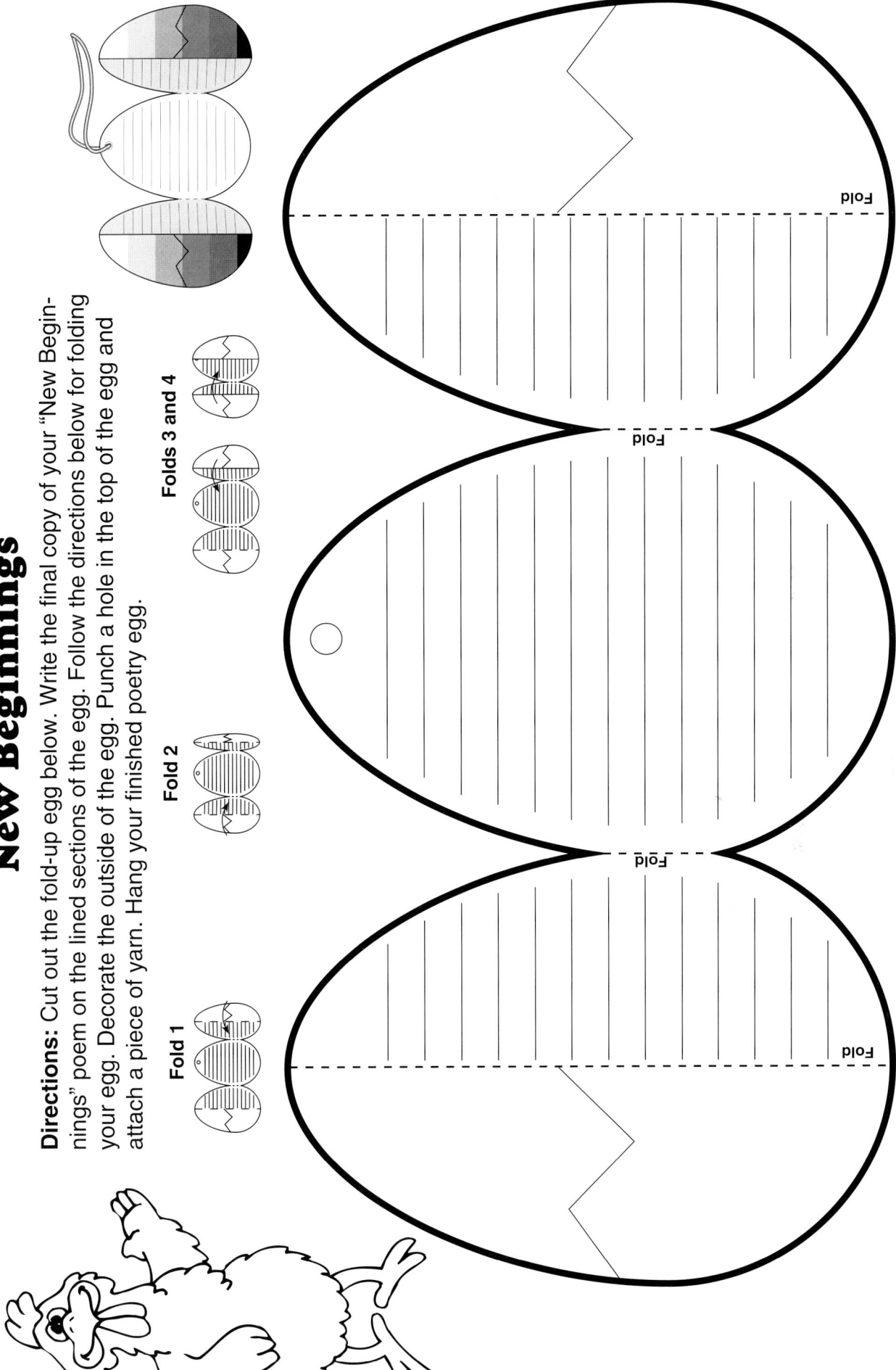

Name _____   *Experiment*

The "Eggs-traordinary" Egg

The egg is made up of four main parts: the shell, the shell membrane, the albumen (or egg white), and the yolk. Follow the directions below to find out more about the egg.

Remember: Wash your hands after touching a raw egg.

Materials needed per group:
- fresh egg
- disposable soup bowl
- 3 craft sticks
- 2 paper towels

Procedure/observations:
Locate and check off each italicized item in the diagram.

1. Observe the *eggshell* from the outside. What do you notice about its color and texture? _____
2. Crack the egg gently on the edge of your teacher's mixing bowl. Empty the contents of the egg into your bowl, and set the shell on a paper towel.
3. Look for the *shell membrane;* the membrane is actually two thin, white membranes that lie very close together.
4. Touch the shell membrane. How does it feel? _____
   What color is it? _____
5. Locate the *albumen* (egg white).
6. Touch the albumen. How does it feel? _____
7. Locate the *yolk*.
8. Touch the yolk gently so that it doesn't break. How does it feel? _____
   What color is it? _____
9. Locate the *air cell, germ-spot,* and *chalazas* (thick, white ropelike structures at each end of the yolk that anchor it to the shell).
10. After you have finished observing all the parts of your egg, break the yolk using a craft stick. Describe what happens. _____

Conclusions:

On the back of this sheet, write a paragraph describing what you learned about the egg from this activity.

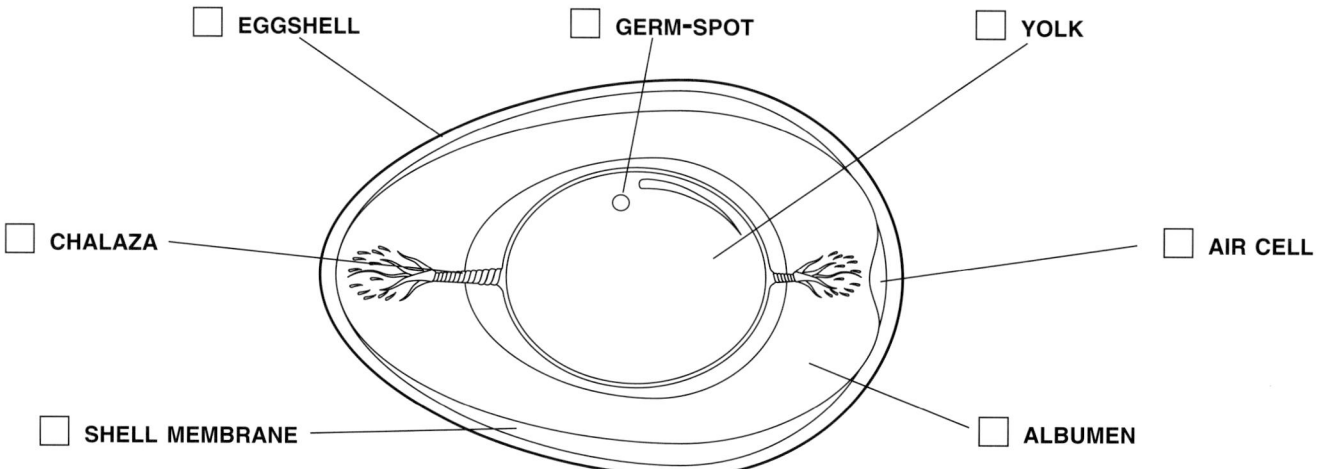

☐ EGGSHELL   ☐ GERM-SPOT   ☐ YOLK
☐ CHALAZA   ☐ AIR CELL
☐ SHELL MEMBRANE   ☐ ALBUMEN

©The Education Center, Inc. • *MARCH* • TEC208

82 **Note to the teacher:** Use with "The 'Eggs-traordinary' Egg" on page 78.

Name _____ Art activity

"Unbe-leaf-able" Eggs

Add a little variety to the traditional method of decorating Easter eggs by making leaf-decorated Easter eggs.

Materials for each student:
- hard-boiled egg
- small leaves
- knee-high stocking
- twist tie
- vinegar
- food coloring
- see-through, 8-oz. cup
- paper towels
- 2-inch section of an empty paper-towel roll
- craft materials

Directions:

1. Go outside with your class and collect small, thin leaves (less than two inches long).

2. Wash the leaves. While they are still wet, press the leaves to the outside of a hard-boiled egg.

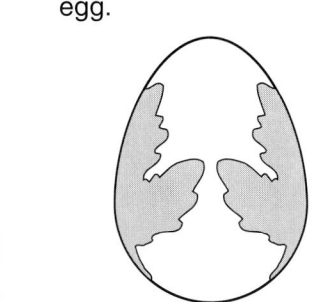

3. Place the egg inside a knee-high stocking. Twist the knee-high and secure the end with a twist tie.

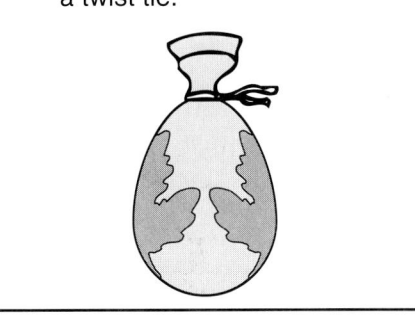

4. Fill the cup with vinegar and add about five drops of food coloring.

5. Soak the egg in vinegar for about 20 minutes or until you are satisfied with the color.

6. Remove the egg from the solution. Set it on a paper towel.

7. Remove the stocking and leaves from the egg. Let the egg dry.

8. Using craft materials, decorate the paper-towel section to make a stand for your egg.

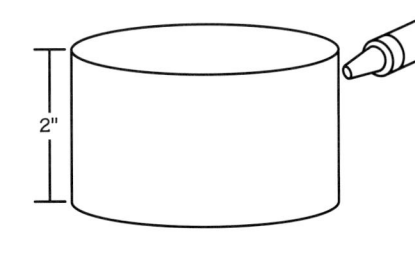

9. Display your "unbe-leaf-able" egg in the school's media center.

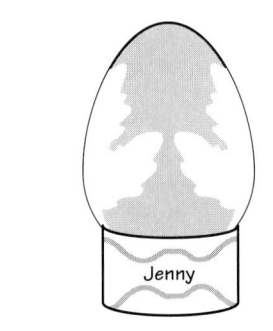

Bonus Box: Research the Ukrainian method of egg decoration known as *pysanky*. Tell how pysanky is different from the process you used to decorate your egg.

©The Education Center, Inc. • *MARCH* • TEC208

Nutrition Nuggets

Action-Packed Activities for Teaching About Nutrition

Serve up this balanced diet of healthful ideas to celebrate National Nutrition Month®!

by Maureen Winkler, Karen Richmond, Janet Radcliffe, and Peggy Hambright

Eat Well and Live Long
Classifying foods, constructing a Food Guide Pyramid

Help students become aware of the foods they consume by introducing the Food Guide Pyramid. Prior to beginning your unit, have each student keep a one-day record of each food she ate and the amount she consumed. Duplicate page 88 for each student. After pointing out the parts of the Food Guide Pyramid, have the student classify each food she ate into one of the pyramid food groups. Then have her construct the Food Pyramid model to use as a reference for "What's on the Menu?" on page 85.

Do You Really Want to Eat That?
Learning about food additives

If you've read a food label, you've probably noticed such words as *monosodium glutamate, BHA, sodium benzoate,* and *citric acid.* Chances are, if you can't identify an ingredient on the food label, it is an additive. When added to foods, these chemicals prevent spoilage or increase the nutrients. Give students a better understanding of the additives in their favorite foods. Ask students to bring in the ingredient labels from a variety of foods. Compile a class list of the unfamiliar ingredients. Then assign one or more of these ingredients to each pair of students. Instruct the pair to record on an index card the additive's identity, what it does for food, and in which foods it can be found. Use the chart on the left as a guide. Collect the cards and bind them into a book titled "You Are What You Eat!"

FOOD ADDITIVES

Types of Additives	What They Do	Examples
Antioxidants	prevent spoilage	butylated hydroxyanisol (BHA), propyl gallate, ascorbic acid (vitamin C)
Preservatives	prevent spoilage	benzoic acid, sorbic acid, sulfur dioxide
Sequestrants	prevent foods from changing color	ethylenediamine tetra-acetate (EDTA), citric acid
Humectants	help retain moisture in foods	glycerol, sorbitol

Fill 'Er Up!
Understanding the importance of good nutrition, writing for a purpose

Are your students running on full tanks, nutritionally speaking? Help them understand the importance of a good diet by sharing this analogy: just as a car runs best on a full tank of gas, the body stays healthier when it is energized from proper eating. Next, challenge each student to keep track of his eating habits over a five-day period. Duplicate the tank pattern on page 87 for each student. Point out that the tank shows only the minimum number of daily servings required for a balanced diet. Direct each student to track the foods he eats each day by checking the appropriate box once he has eaten the minimum daily servings of that food group. Then have him evaluate how well he kept his body's tank full by completing the bottom chart. On the back of his pattern, instruct the student to write three things he will do in the coming week to either maintain his good eating habits or change his bad ones.

What's on the Menu?
Understanding and using a Food Guide Pyramid

Help Nell the Nutty Nutritionist plan meals for Mrs. Wanda B. Healthy for a week. Divide your class into seven groups; then assign each group a day of the week. Using the USDA's Food Guide Pyramid (see the pattern on page 88), have each group plan breakfast, lunch, dinner, and two snacks for Wanda to eat on the assigned day. After the meals and snacks have been planned, supply the groups with old magazines and art materials. Then instruct each group to design a large, creative, and colorful menu that promotes the meals and snacks it planned. Post the menus on a bulletin board titled "Menus for Mrs. Wanda B. Healthy." For a fun border, let students contribute magazine cutouts of healthful foods and snacks to staple around the board's perimeter.

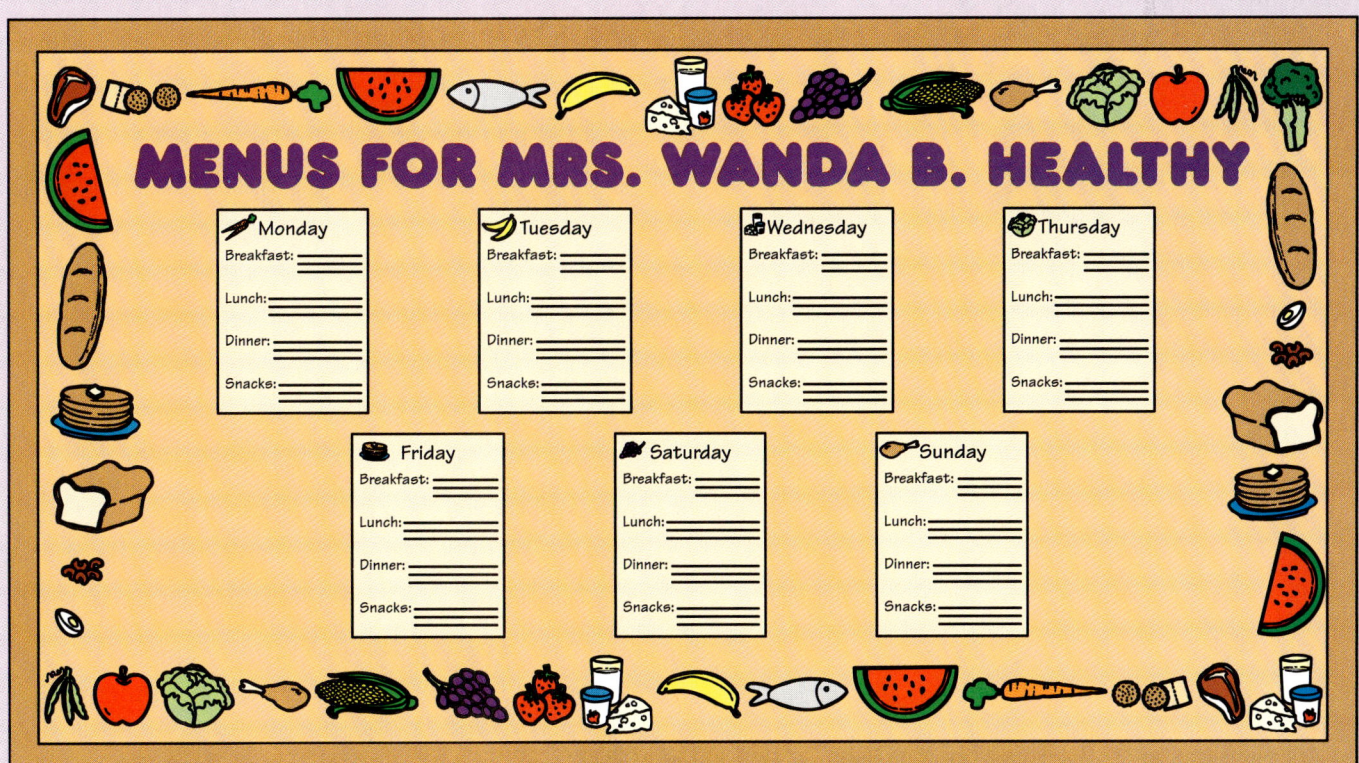

Nell's Edible Plants
Categorizing foods

Would you care for some crispy roots or tender stems for lunch? How about a tasty flower or a crunchy seed for dinner? Discover if students really know what they eat by playing a fun, interactive game. Write the following categories on chart paper: Fruit, Seed, Flower, Leaf, Root, and Stem. Leave room under each category for students to place Post-it® Brand notes. Next, write the name of each vegetable listed on the chart on a Post-it® Brand note. Then randomly stick the notes to a vegetable stand drawn on the chalkboard.

Divide students into two teams. In turn, choose one person from a team to go to the board, pull one vegetable note from the stand, and place it under one of the categories. If the vegetable is categorized correctly, award the team one point. If done incorrectly, have the student return the note to the stand. Call on the next team and continue play. When all the vegetables have been grouped under the correct headings, add up the points to see which team knows its plants!

Fruit	Seed	Flower
eggplant	pea	broccoli
sweet pepper	lima bean	cauliflower
tomato	snap bean	
	corn	

Leaf	Root	Stem
cabbage	potato	celery
lettuce	beet	asparagus
parsley	radish	mushroom
brussels sprout	turnip	
spinach	carrot	
	onion	

The War of the Nutrients
Understanding the importance of nutrients, writing for a purpose

Of all the chemicals we consume, only six main groups of nutrients are essential to keep us healthy. The nutrients *water, carbohydrates, fats,* and *proteins* are needed by our bodies in large quantities. On the other hand, we only need small amounts of the nutrients *minerals* and *vitamins*. Combine writing skills and nutrition facts by staging a battle of words. Divide the class into six groups. Assign each group one of the six main groups of nutrients and challenge each group to prove why that nutrient is the most important. After researching the nutrient, have the group write four paragraphs—a *descriptive* paragraph outlining the benefits of the nutrient, an *expository* paragraph that tells how to obtain the good benefits of the nutrient (which foods to eat and in what quantities), a *clarification* paragraph that gives the reasons why this nutrient should be recognized as the most important nutrient, and a *persuasive* paragraph to gather support for consuming that nutrient. Have each group bind its completed, edited paragraphs between two covers. Display all six reports on a wall under the heading "The Super Six."

The Healthful-Eating Campaign
Researching nutrition-related topics

Help others learn more about healthful eating habits by creating informational visuals. Divide students into groups of three or four. Give each group one of the topics below to research. Have each group present its research in the form of a poster, mobile, brochure, or picture book.

Display the projects in the cafeteria, hallways, media center, or other high-traffic areas. Encourage other classes to visit the display. Then congratulate your students for having planted the seeds of healthful-eating habits throughout the school.

- the number of calories in favorite snacks
- the amounts of fat and cholesterol in favorite foods
- how to read nutrition labels
- foods that help prevent cancer
- foods that are low in cholesterol
- the whys and hows of vitamins
- what the labels *low fat, fat free, light,* and *lean* really mean

My Nutrition Tank
(Minimum Number of Daily Food Group Servings)

Use the charts below to keep track of your eating habits for five days. On each day that you eat the minimum daily requirement, check the box next to that food group.

Food Group (servings per day)	Mon.	Tues.	Wed.	Thurs.	Fri.
Fats (use sparingly)					
Milk (2 servings)					
Meat (2 servings)					
Vegetables (3 servings)					
Fruit (2 servings)					
Bread (6 servings)					

Today my tank was	full	half full	almost empty
Monday			
Tuesday			
Wednesday			
Thursday			
Friday			

Name:
Date:

Note to the teacher: Make one copy of this pattern for each student to use with "Fill 'Er Up!" on page 85. Students will need their constructed Food Guide Pyramids from page 88 to complete the activity.

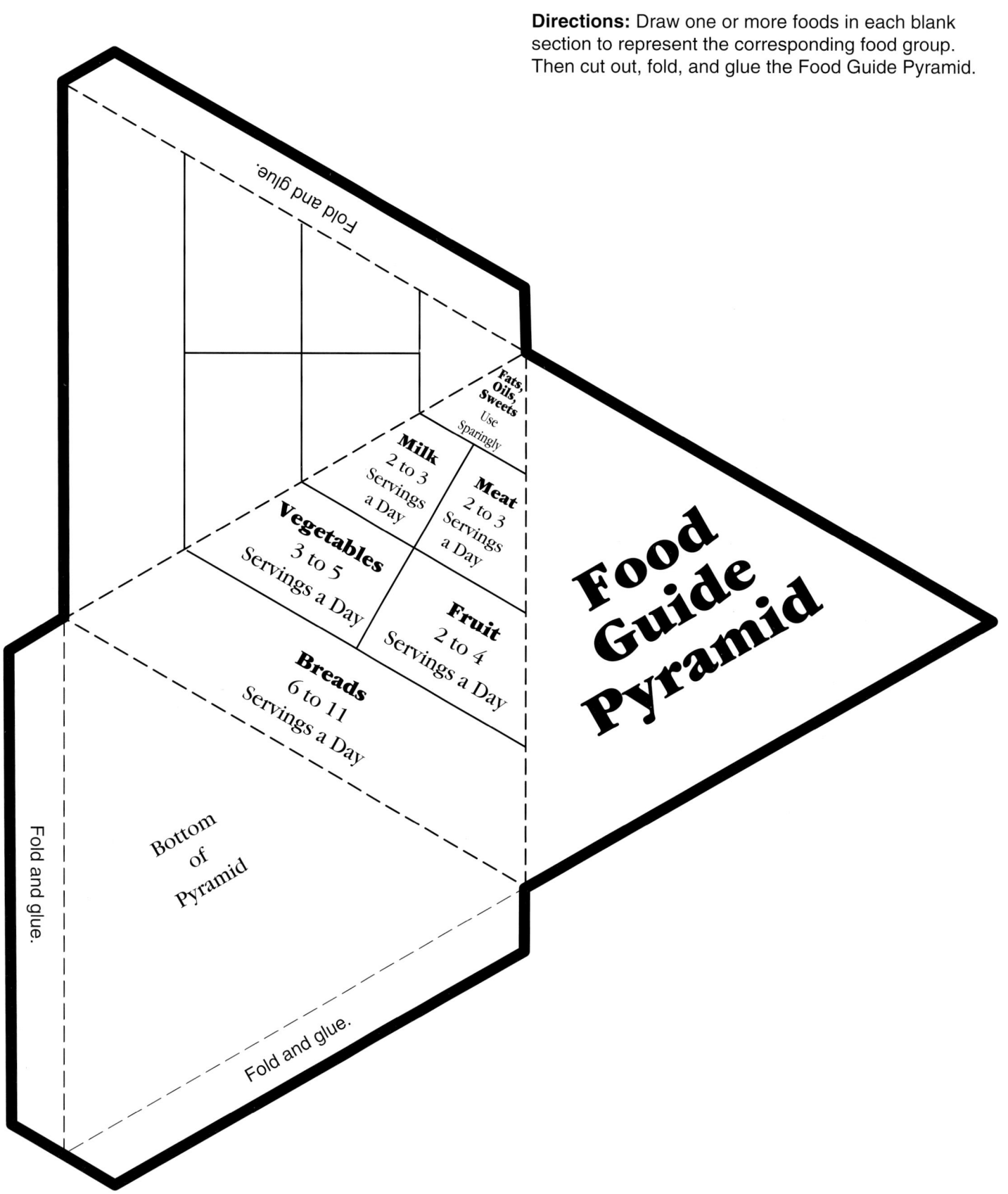

Name _____

Student-activity calendar

Daily Doses of Nutrition

For the Month of _____

Complete one activity each day. Store your work in a folder. Hand in the folder at the end of the month.

MONDAY	TUESDAY	WEDNESDAY	THURSDAY	FRIDAY
Do you think that eating sweets for snacks is a good idea? Why or why not?	For each letter in *nutrition*, write one adjective to describe an unhealthful food.	Write an acrostic poem about *nutrition* that will encourage others to eat properly.	List three goals you can set to make sure your body gets the nutrients it needs.	Write a good response to give a friend who teases you about eating properly.
Organize the information in the USDA's Food Guide Pyramid in a different shape.	List as many healthful foods as you can that begin with the letters in *Food Guide Pyramid*.	Invent a new vitamin. Describe how it helps the body and name foods that contain it.	Invent a new vegetable. Explain the benefits of including this new veggie in your diet.	Are you more likely to eat healthful foods if they are colorful? Why or why not?
What is the most important meal of the day to you? Why?	Why is it sometimes difficult to teach people to eat foods that are good for them?	Write a three- to five-step plan to improve your eating habits.	What could you say to a friend who eats too much junk food?	Use adjectives to describe a food in detail without mentioning the food by name.
From which food group do you eat the most servings a day? Why?	List two reasons that your best friend should not eat many servings from the fats, oils, and sweets group.	Name five healthful after-school snacks.	Write the names of five to ten vegetables that can be made into juices.	Why do you think breakfast is such an important meal?
Name five healthful foods that begin with the letter *p*.	Describe three creative ways to include vegetables in your diet.	What did you eat for breakfast this morning? Was it a healthful choice? Why or why not?	Write the names of five vegetables, five fruits, and two meats, scrambling the letters that spell each word. Make a key.	How have you changed your eating habits since beginning our nutrition unit?

©The Education Center, Inc. • MARCH • TEC208

Note to the teacher: Use this calendar at the beginning of the month during your nutrition unit. Fill in the name of the month and each day's date in the corner of its box before making a class set. Give each student one copy of this page and a pocketed folder. Have the student complete one activity each day and store his work inside the folder. Collect the folders on the last day of the month.

Name_____   *Nutrition and geography*

States of Nutrition ☆☆☆☆☆

A well-balanced diet depends on the year-round production of food products. Several states in the United States lead in producing fruits and vegetables and in raising dairy and beef cattle. Draw the following symbols on a U.S. map inside the states listed below.

🌽	**CORN**	OH, IN, IL, IA, MO, KS, NE
🌾	**WHEAT**	ND, KS, MT, OK
🥬	**LETTUCE**	CA, OR, WA, AZ, CO, MA, NY, NJ, NC, SC, FL
🍊	**ORANGES**	FL, CA, TX, AZ
🍋	**GRAPEFRUIT**	FL, CA, AZ, TX
🍋	**LEMONS**	CA, AZ, FL
🍎	**APPLES**	WA, NY, MI, CA, PA, VA
🐂	**BEEF CATTLE**	TX, MO, OK, NE, SD, MT, KS, IA, KY, FL
🐄	**DAIRY CATTLE**	WI, CA, NY, MN, PA, TX, MI, OH, IA

Then use the map to find the state or states that

1. produce both corn and dairy cattle. _____

2. lead in both beef cattle and dairy cattle. _____

3. leads only in the production of wheat. _____

4. is a one-word northeastern state that produces lettuce. _____

5. leads in producing the most products in the West. _____

6. is in the midwest region and produces beef cattle and wheat but not corn. _____

7. produce apples and border a Great Lake. _____

8. lead in the production of dairy cattle, apples, and lettuce. _____

9. is one of three states that lead in the production of corn but not beef cattle. _____

10. is in the southeast region and produces lemons. _____

Bonus Box: Color the state in which you live. On the back of this sheet, list all the products and goods that your state produces. Select one product or good, and write a sentence describing why that product is important to the citizens of your state.

©The Education Center, Inc. • *MARCH* • TEC208 • Key p. 93

90 **Note to the teacher:** Make one copy of this sheet and the U.S. map on page 91 for each student.

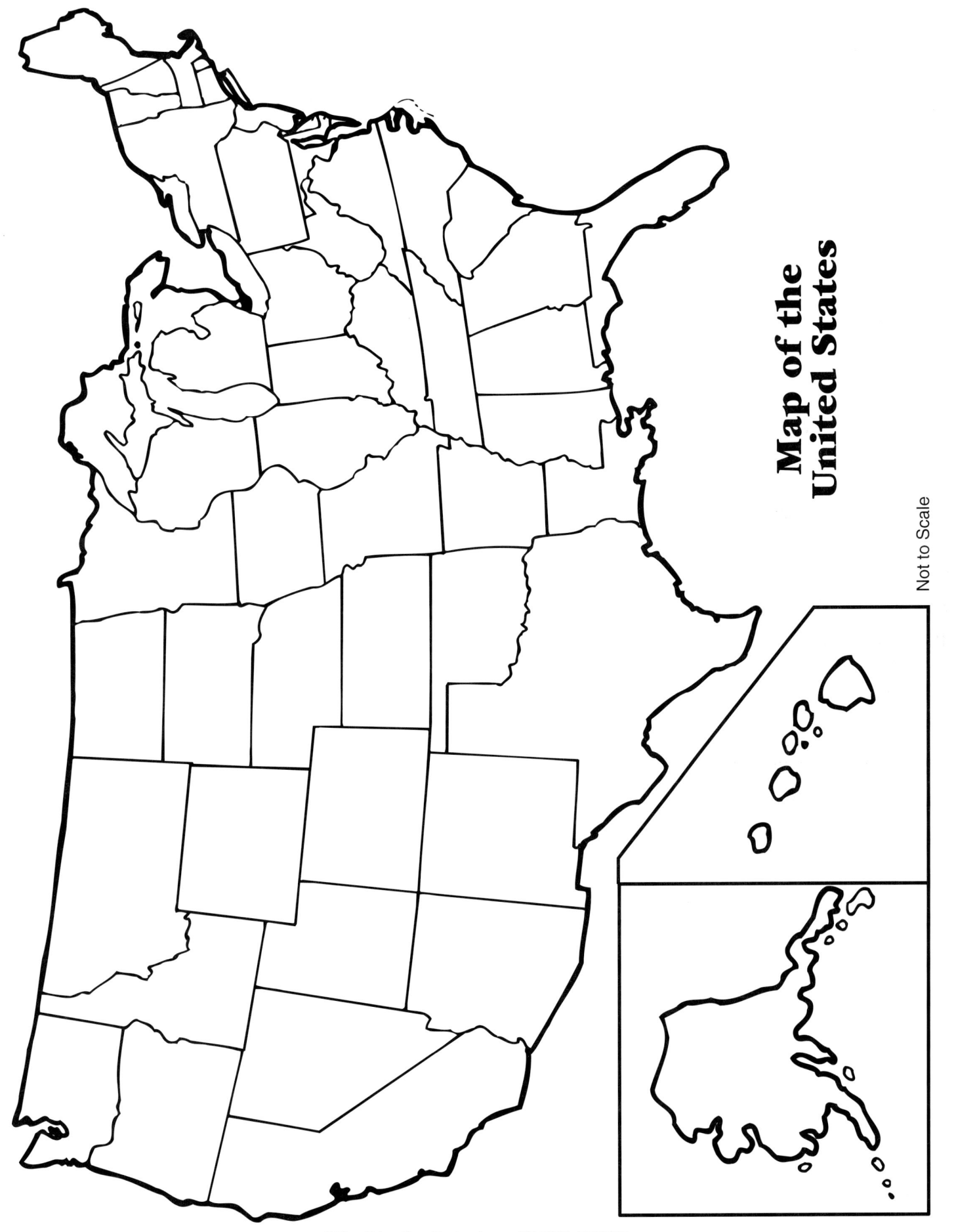

Note to the teacher: Use this map with "States of Nutrition" on page 90. Make one copy for each student.

Answer Keys

Page 17
1. $71.40
2. $1.29
3. $5.40
4. $27.92
5. $5.09
6. $4.75
7. Total is $55.50. Possible combination: two $20 bills, one $10 bill, one $5 bill, and one $1 bill. The change will be $0.50.
8. $9.85
9. two
10. $49.50
11. $13.32
12. $19.95

Page 24
1. MW for Martha Washington
2. JK or JKO for Jacqueline Kennedy (Onassis)
3. ER for Eleanor Roosevelt
4. ER for Eleanor Roosevelt
5. BB for Barbara Bush
6. DM for Dolley Madison
7. AA for Abigail Adams
8. JK or JKO for Jacqueline Kennedy (Onassis)
9. ER for Eleanor Roosevelt
10. BB for Barbara Bush
11. HRC for Hillary Rodham Clinton
12. NR for Nancy Reagan
13. MW for Martha Washington
14. BB for Barbara Bush
15. AA for Abigail Adams
16. HRC for Hillary Rodham Clinton

Page 36
Part A: Observations will vary. Students should observe that each measurement is different. They should conclude that units based on persons' measurements will not be consistent because not everyone is the same size.

Bonus Box:
A knot measures a ship's speed in nautical miles per hour.
A fathom is a unit used to measure the depth of water.
  1 fathom = 6 feet.
A watt measures the power used to light a bulb.
A speedometer measures the speed traveled by
  a vehicle.
An odometer measures the distance traveled by a vehicle.

Page 37
1 foot = 12 inches
1 yard = 3 feet or 36 inches
1 mile = 5,280 feet or 1,760 yards
1 centimeter = 10 millimeters
1 decimeter = 10 centimeters or 100 millimeters
1 meter = 100 centimeters or 10 decimeters
1 kilometer = 1,000 meters
2 feet = 24 inches
2 yards = 6 feet or 72 inches
2 decimeters = 20 centimeters or 200 millimeters
2 meters = 200 centimeters or 20 decimeters
2 kilometers = 2,000 meters
5 decimeters = 50 centimeters or 500 millimeters
5 meters = 500 centimeters or 50 decimeters
5 kilometers = 5,000 meters

Page 40
1. bull shark
2. humpback whale
3. killer whale
4. tiger shark
5. scalloped hammerhead shark
6. spinner dolphin
7. bottle-nosed dolphin
8. striped dolphin
9. blue whale
10. white shark
11. striped dolphin
12. blue whale
13. bottle-nosed dolphin and bull shark
14. spinner dolphin and bull shark
15. bull shark

Bonus Box: 273 ft. 9 in.

Page 41
Answers will vary. After each student completes each activity one time, he will have 55 minutes and 4 tickets left over. He will still need to use the last 4 tickets and eat lunch.

Bonus Box: The student can fit five activities into two hours. The number of tickets will vary with the activities chosen.

Page 43
1. THE SNACK BAR
2. ELBOW PADS
3. GET SOME PIZZA
4. MY COUSIN JERRY
5. BY FIVE

Page 51
1. Valentine's Day
2. Italy
3. eating
4. song
5. slate
6. nonfiction
7. ground
8. blue
9. jam
10. Mexico, Spain, or other Spanish-speaking country
11. St. Patrick's Day
12. instrument
13. Thanksgiving
14. Washington, DC
15. wood

Page 52
Lenny's job is decorating.
Larry's job is invitations.
Leo's job is shopping.
Luther's job is cooking.
Laura's job is cleaning.
Lois's job is music.

Page 61

	Dublin	Limerick	Kilkenny	Tipperary	McMurphy	McNamara	O'Leary	O'Mally
Tom	O	X	X	X	X	X	O	X
Patrick	X	X	X	O	O	X	X	X
Stephen	X	X	O	X	X	O	X	X
Sean	X	O	X	X	X	X	X	O
McMurphy	X	X	X	O				
McNamara	X	X	O	X				
O'Leary	O	X	X	X				
O'Mally	X	O	X	X				

Page 53

1) Six students believe in Santa Claus only; 18 students believe in leprechauns only.

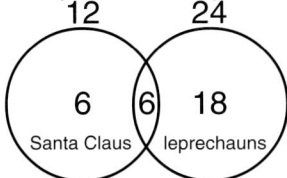

2) Thirteen students knew only what he was famous for; nine students knew only his job; seven students knew only where he was born.

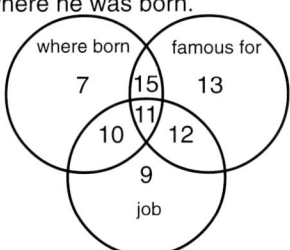

3) Twelve companies donated equipment; six companies donated refreshments; ten companies donated uniforms.

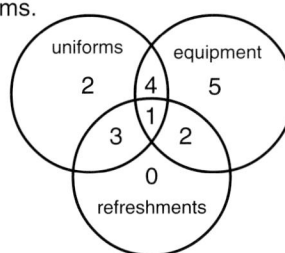

4) Thirty-six people only wear green; 29 people only attend parades; 27 people only attend religious ceremonies.

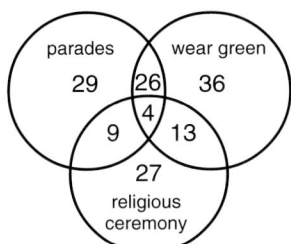

Bonus Box: 3

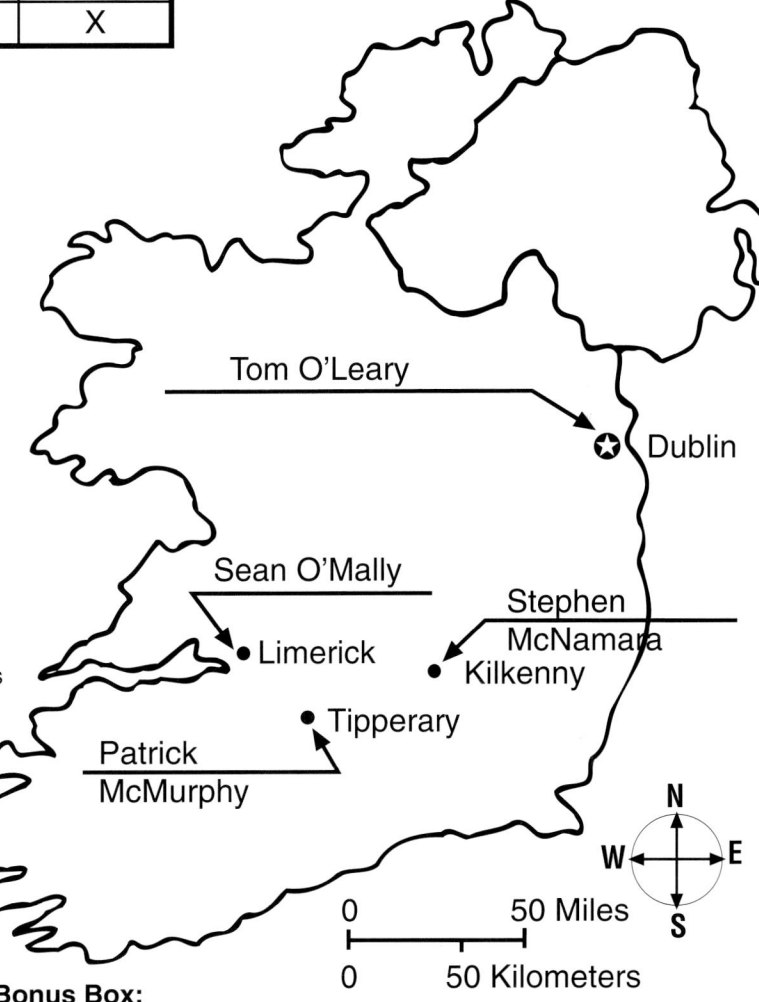

Bonus Box:
Tom O'Leary lives in the capital city.
Sean O'Mally = approximately 110 miles
Stephen McNamara = approximately 70 miles
Patrick McMurphy = approximately 100 miles

Page 90
1. OH or IA
2. TX and IA
3. ND
4. MA
5. CA
6. OK
7. MI, NY, or PA
8. CA and NY
9. OH, IN, or IL
10. FL

Index

American Red Cross Month (see also Health)
    research, 4
Animals
    eggs, 76–83
    ocean, 40
Art Appreciation
    Michelangelo, 5
    Youth Art Month, 5
Arts and Crafts
    baskets, 11
    collage, 31, 33
    dye, 83
    Easter eggs, 83
    faces, 31
    flowers, 67
    illustration, 5, 12, 18, 46, 64, 66, 68
    paper dolls, 21
    person, 33
    pot of gold, 54
    prints, 66
    pyramid, 84
    sculpture, grass, 69
Authors
    female, 23
    Silverstein, Shel, 65
Bell, Alexander Graham
    birthday, 4
Biographical Writing
    female athletes, 22
Birthdays
    Bell, Alexander Graham, 4
    Frost, Robert, 13
    Michelangelo, 5
Bookmaking
    alphabet, 67
    nutrition, 84, 86
    plants, 67
Books
    The Giving Tree, 65
Bulletin Boards and Displays
    athletes, female, 22
    eggs, 76, 77
    Ireland, 54, 57
    math, 34
    music, 19
    nutrition, 87
    poetry, 77
    poets, female, 22
    reading, 45
    spring, 8, 10
    student art, 31, 34
    student writing, 8, 10, 45, 46, 57, 76, 77, 87
    trees, 65
Character Education
    community service, 11
    contributions of others, 13, 19, 20, 22, 23
    goals and objectives, 13
    kindness, 45
    National Procrastination Week, 4
    responsibility, 4
Classifying (see Critical Thinking)

Classroom Management
    tips for spring, 9
Clothing
    women's fashion, 21
Code (see Logic)
Community Service (see Character Education)
Comparative Writing
    Ireland, 57
Compare and Contrast (see Critical Thinking)
Contracts, Learning
    nutrition, 89
    spring, 16
    St. Patrick's Day, 50
    women's history, 28
Cooking
    Potato Cakes, 47
    Potato Soup, 47
    Soda Farls, 55
Cooperative Groups
    collecting and graphing data, 55
    educators, 21
    graphing, 55
    measurement, 32, 42
    nutrition, 87
    poster, 21
    writing, 57, 87
Crafts (see Arts and Crafts)
Creative Writing
    invention, 4
    Ireland, 56
    mythology, 12
    vocabulary, 12
Critical Thinking
    classifying, 65, 84, 86
    compare and contrast, 57
    opinion, forming an, 18
    planning and strategizing, 4, 5, 56, 85
    patterns and relationships, 21
    plants, 63
    problem solving, 44
Cultural Traditions
    Ireland, 47, 55
Dictionary Skills (see Vocabulary)
Displays (see Bulletin Boards and Displays)
Ecology
    recycling, 80
Eggs
    thematic unit, 76–83
English (see Language Arts)
Environment (see Ecology)
Estimation
    marshmallows, 55
Family Involvement
    plants, 75
Figurative Language
    Irish sayings, 46
Food (see also Cooking)
    nutrition, 84–91
Fractions
    measurement, 43
    reproducible, 43

Frank, Anne
  critical thinking, 5
Free Time
  calendar of activities, 6
  nutrition, 89
Games
  bingo, 33
  bowling, 34
  matching, 23, 86
  memory, 42
  nutrition, 86
  review, 34, 80
  scavenger hunts, 32, 80
  spelling, 78
  vocabulary, 12, 77
Giving Tree, The
  Shel Silverstein, 65
Graphing
  area and perimeter, 34
  collecting and organizing data, 48, 55
  recording data, 57
Health
  National Nutrition Month, 84–91
  nutrition, 84–91
  safety, 4
History
  clothing, 21
  timeline, 20
  women's history, 18–29
  World War II, 5
Holidays and Celebrations (see also Birthdays)
  American Red Cross Month, 4
  National Nutrition Month, 84–91
  National Procrastination Week, 4
  National Weights and Measures Week, 30–43
  National Women's History Month, 18–29
  Newspapers in Education Week, 4
  resource calendar, 6
  St. Patrick's Day, 44–61
  Youth Art Month, 5
Inventors and Inventions
  Bell, Alexander Graham, 4
  Slinky®, 4
Ireland
  St. Patrick's Day, 44–53
  thematic unit, 54–61
Kindness (see Character Education)
Language Arts (see also Books, Poetry, Writing)
  analogies, 51
  dictionary skills, 12
  figurative language, 46, 56
  folklore, 46
  oral communication, 18
  reading, 11
  spelling, 78
  vocabulary, 12, 77
Learning Centers
  language arts, 77
Letter Writing
  editor, 44
  educators, 21
  thank-you, 65

Library Skills
  research, 4, 5, 14, 15, 72
Literature (see also Authors, Books, Poetry, Reading)
  mythology, 12
Logic
  analogies, 51
  code, 43
  puzzle, 52, 61
  reproducible, 52, 53, 61
  Venn diagrams, 53
Making Personal Connections
  new beginnings, 77
  spring, 8
  women, 18
Math
  estimation, 55
  fractions, 43
  graphing, 34, 48, 55, 57
  logic, 43, 52, 61
  measurement, 30–43
  money, 17
Measurement
  National Weights and Measures Week, 30–43
  reproducible, 40, 41, 42, 43
  thematic unit, 30–43
  theodolite, 35
Michelangelo
  birthday, 5
Money
  problem solving, 17
Mythology (see Literature)
National Nutrition Month (see Health)
National Procrastination Week (see Character Education)
National Weights and Measures Week (see Measurement)
National Women's History Month
  thematic unit, 18–29
Newspapers
  Newspapers in Education Week, 4
  parts of, 4
  writing, 4, 79
Nutrition (see Health)
Ocean
  animals, 40
Opinion, Forming an (see Critical Thinking)
Oral Communication
  discussion, 18
  persuasive, 56
  presentation, 21, 56
Patterns
  bingo card, 37
  calendar, 89
  coin, 48
  eggs, 81
  music note, 25
  pyramid, 88
  sailboat, 14
  shamrock, 49
  star, 25
  United States map, 91
Persuasive Writing
  nutrition, 86
Planning and Strategizing (see Critical Thinking)

Plants
- compost, 69
- geotropism, 62
- germination, 63
- thematic unit, 62–75

Poetry
- haiku, 68
- new beginnings, 77
- poets, female, 22
- writing, 13, 22, 68

Reading (see also Authors, Books, Literature)
- motivation, 11, 45
- responding to literature, 23, 45

Recipes (see Cooking)

Reproducibles
- activity calendar, 89
- analogies, 51
- art activity, 83
- famous American women, 28–29
- logic, 52, 61
- measurement, 40–43
- nutrition, 90
- plants, 75
- problem solving, 17, 53
- seasonal contract, 16
- St. Patrick's Day, 50

Research Skills
- athletes, female, 22
- disasters, 4
- educators, female, 21
- eggs, 79
- fashions, women's, 21
- first ladies, 18
- Ireland, 54, 56, 57
- nutrition, 87
- planets, 5
- plants, 64, 67
- poets, female, 22
- seasons, 10
- singers, 19
- women's rights, 20

Responsibility (see Character Education)

Review and Recall
- concepts and skills, 80
- goals and objectives, 13
- spelling words, 78
- vocabulary, 77

Safety (see Health)

Science (see also Animals, Health)
- classification, 65
- ecology, 80
- experiments, 62, 63, 68, 69, 70, 78
- making a model, 67
- observation skills, 10, 64, 66
- ocean, 40
- plants, 62–75, 80
- seasons, 8, 10, 12
- space, 5
- time, 5
- weather, 13, 57

Seasons
- spring, 8–17

Silverstein, Shel
- *The Giving Tree,* 65

Social Studies (see also Character Education, History)
- agriculture, United States, 90
- Ireland, 54–61
- reproducible, 90

Space
- planets, 5

Spelling
- review game, 78

Spring
- thematic unit, 8–17

St. Patrick's Day
- thematic unit, 44–61

Student Motivation
- spring, 9
- reading, 11, 45
- writing, 76

Time
- daylight saving time, 5
- measuring elapsed, 41
- reproducible, 41
- timelines, 20

Venn Diagrams (see Logic)

Vocabulary
- dictionary skills, 12
- games, 12, 77
- stumpers, 12

Weather
- climate, 57
- wind, 13

Writing
- biographical, 22
- comparative, 57
- creative, 4, 12
- explanatory, 10
- for a purpose, 4, 12, 21, 22, 44, 45, 46, 63, 64, 65, 67, 79, 85, 86
- letters, 21, 44, 65
- narrative, 56
- poetry, 13, 22, 68, 77

Youth Art Month (see Art Appreciation)